Las Vegas

D0967583

An architectural guide

•••

Frances Anderton and John Chase
Photographs by Keith Collie

Las Vegas

An architectural guide

●●● **ellipsis KÖNEMANN**

•••

CREATED, EDITED AND DESIGNED BY
Ellipsis London Limited
55 Charlotte Road London EC2A 3QT
E MAIL ...@ellipsis.co.uk
WWW http://www.ellipsis.co.uk/ellipsis
PUBLISHED IN THE UK AND AFRICA BY
Ellipsis London Limited
SERIES EDITOR Tom Neville
EDITOR Annie Bridges
SERIES DESIGN Jonathan Moberly
LAYOUT Pauline Harrison

COPYRIGHT © 1997 Könemann
Verlagsgesellschaft mbH
Bonner Str. 126, D-50968 Köln
PRODUCTION MANAGER Detlev Schaper
PRINTING AND BINDING Sing Cheong
Printing Ltd
Printed in Hong Kong

ISBN 3 89508 639 8 (Könemann)
ISBN 1 899858 14 8 (Ellipsis)
10 9 8 7 6 5 4 3 2

Frances Anderton and John Chase 1996

Contents

Introduction 6

Acknowledgements 17

How to use this book 16

The Strip and Downtown 19

South-east Las Vegas 109

South-west Las Vegas 155

North-east Las Vegas 177

North-west Las Vegas 187

Outside Las Vegas 205

Index 213

Introduction

There are plenty of other places in the US where tourists can gamble besides Las Vegas. Visitors choose to go there because the city is a legend. When you think of Las Vegas you don't just think of casinos; you think of Elvis, Sinatra, Howard Hughes, the drug-crazed Hunter Thompson, showgirls and hookers, blinding neon and champagne-bubble twinkle lights. Las Vegas is the first place any self-respecting student of the built environment would go to in the US to find white-hot visual excitement combined with the all-purpose moral licence to enjoy it.

It is also the last place on the face of the earth where you would expect to find architecture that deserves to be included in a guidebook on the grounds of architectural merit alone. This is because the visual excitement of Las Vegas is not derived primarily from its architecture.

During daylight hours the city skyline is dominated by the hulking presence of the hotel casinos, most of which are undistinguished late-modern dormitory-like blocks. Made from steel frame and concrete panel and thrown up at astonishing speed, the casinos are generally low-lit, low-ceilinged warrens jam-packed with gaming facilities. There are no windows, no clocks, and the exits are obscured. The aim behind the design of these casinos is, simply, to expose people to the maximum number of revenue-producing entities – opportunities to gamble – in as entertaining a way as possible.

By night the fabled neon and flashing lights bring Las Vegas alive: Bally's brutish twin towers fluoresce in a cobalt-blue glow, and the vast Caesars hotel block with its attendant *porte-cochère*, monstrous by day, glows electric pink and green, an other-worldly fantasia. Day or night, scintillating textures, patterns, colours and themes give character to the casino interiors. The full glory of the Las Vegas casino is the product not of individual firms but of teams of architects, sign and show designers, and interior designers whose artistry has elevated it, within the culture of art and architecture, to the level of pop icon.

But closer investigation reveals a fast-developing city which can now boast some interesting examples of 'high-art' architecture alongside an evolving casino architecture. The real Las Vegas has jumped from 200,000 to 1 million inhabitants in 20 years, and it is generating culture at the same time as it is trying to keep pace with the traffic, pollution, homelessness and other urban ills that such rapid success brings.

Architecture is taking on a greater importance in Las Vegas, which is now spawning civic and cultural buildings. In recent years public monies have been spent on an ambitious library-building programme, as well as on various street improvement projects. A huge sports stadium and a new late modern-style courthouse (by Dworsky Asociates/Harry Campbell Architects) are planned for the downtown area, and high-tech mass transit systems are under consideration.

The casinos, once defined by their neon spectaculars, have become in themselves spectacles. The new family-oriented destination resorts that have sprung up on the Strip, such as Excalibur, Luxor and Treasure Island, have a monumentality and architectural presence, albeit of a stage-set variety, that reflects the increasing significance of the architect and, furthermore, the show designer. They, rather than the sign designer, are becoming increasingly responsible for defining the image of the Strip.

We have gone beyond the Strip, taking an inclusive look at the resort district and the supporting communities around it that constitute the contemporary city. We have sought out the architectural nuggets that do exist, in a city whose building stock has traditionally been utilitarian and where emphasis, in both casino and non-casino architecture, has been on speed and cheapness. And we have included the work of both new and more established architectural firms in the public and private sectors, who are attempting to raise the stature of architecture in a city where the largest firm has only 13 licensed architects, and where traditional public antipathy to taxes has led to a diminished public domain.

Las Vegas is located in the southern tip of the state of Nevada on flat, unyielding terrain between mountain ranges that separate it from the natural desert wonders of Death Valley, to the west in California, and the Grand Canyon, to the east in Arizona.

Characterised by baking hot summers (110 degrees Fahrenheit is normal) and windy winters, separated by the short beautiful spells of fall and spring, it is an essentially hostile environment. Las Vegas owes its existence, initially, to the presence of water, in the shape of artesian wells that enabled early habitation, and, later, to power, in the form of the nearby man-made spectacular, the Hoover Dam (formerly Boulder Dam).

The city barely existed before the turn of the century. The area was inhabited by a series of Indian tribes, most recently the Southern Paiute, and by Spanish explorers who named it 'Las Vegas', meaning 'the meadows'. From the mid-nineteenth century a wagon route passed through, bringing Mormon settlers and, later, supplies for western mines. In 1902 a midroute supply depot for the Los Angeles and Salt Lake Railroad was established there; this brought in additional Mormon settlers who would subsequently invest in the city's future.

And then Uncle Sam stepped in: first in 1928, when Las Vegas was selected as the site for the Depression-era engineering marvel, the Hoover Dam, and then again in wartime when Vegas became the location for the Nellis Airforce Base, test-base for Thunderbirds, Stealth Fighters and Bombers, and provider of thousands of new residents. In the 1950s, the US military further expanded its presence in the area, selecting a site 50 miles north of Vegas for nuclear tests. These tests proved a boon rather than a dampener for the burgeoning tourist industry as imaginative casino owners offered gambling guests the added thrill of atom-bomb-viewing breakfasts and other spectacles.

In 1931 the State of Nevada legalised gambling, and control of Las Vegas fell into the hands of enterprising individuals and mobsters, personified by such figures as Benjamin 'Bugsy' Siegel of Murder, Inc., who arrived from the East Coast via LA in the 1940s and took over Billy Wilkerson's Flamingo in 1946. This chic casino started the trend for Los Angeles-style modern glamour, which replaced the nostalgic Western imagery that had previously characterised resort architecture. Twenty years after 'Bugsy' came Jay Sarno, creator of the themed Caesars Palace and the family-oriented Circus Circus in the mid-1960s.

Las Vegas remained a pleasant resort and gambling town, operating under the benevolent tyranny of local toughs, until purges of the criminal element took place in the 1960s.

In 1967 Howard Hughes, the reclusive billionaire, made his entry into Las Vegas. Having outstayed his welcome at the Desert Inn, he bought the whole hotel and went on to buy $300 million of Las Vegas property that included the Sands, Castaways, the Frontier, the Silver Slipper, the North Las Vegas Airport and a TV station. Hughes' casino spending spree paved the way for the Nevada Corporate Gaming Acts of 1967 and 1969 which allowed publicly traded corporations to acquire gambling licences. This stimulated an unprecedented property speculation boom and led to the corporatisation of gambling and the city's high-rise skyline.

Deregulation in the 1970s and 1980s further accelerated the city's growth and gave rise to present-day Las Vegas, where predominantly corporate-controlled casinos, of ever-increasing scale, sell sanitised vice

Las Vegas: a guide to recent architecture

and Disney-inspired themed family entertainment to an ever-increasing number of visitors.

The late 1980s saw the emergence of the entrepreneurial Steve Wynn, founder of the Mirage and Treasure Island, who, together with William Bennett of Excalibur, initiated the trend away from the adult-oriented casino-hotel to the family-oriented, themed, mega-entertainment resort.

Las Vegas' rapid growth has resulted in a city that has catered largely to itinerant workers and gamblers, leaving a legacy of hurriedly-built, serviceable residential and civic buildings, but virtually no public domain. With tourism on the rise (almost 30 million visitors per year and eight new mega-resorts promising 20,000 more hotel rooms under way), so too is the local population, resulting in dramatic physical changes in scale of both the gambling tourist centre and the surrounding city.

Despite its rapid growth, Las Vegas is still a relatively small place, manageable in two or three days. The city is conveniently divided north–south by Las Vegas Boulevard (the Strip) and east–west by another large commercial highway, Charleston Boulevard. The buildings in this guide are thus neatly subdivided into six sections: the Strip and Downtown/Fremont Street, which contains most of the casinos and resort buildings; North-west (anything north-west of the Strip and Charleston Boulevard); North-east, South-east; South-west, and outside the city.

The buildings in the Strip area are arranged in the order you would see them if, as is usual, you approach Las Vegas from Interstate-15 or the airport. This is a stunning entry, especially at night, and, initially, is best made in a car so as to fully experience the drive-by visual bombardment that blasts you on emerging from the quiet of a long trip through the desert. This route will take you back in time, first past the most recent of the Las Vegas casino/mega-resorts, the dramatic Luxor, the MGM

Grand and the Excalibur. Making their presence felt in monumental, theatrical buildings and streetside spectacles, they give a first taste of the new family-oriented, themed resorts that are now redefining the character of the gambling district. Then northwards, past Steve Wynn's influential Treasure Island and the Mirage, past the seminal Caesars Palace and on to the older part of town, Fremont Street. This domestic-scale street of casinos, known worldwide for its glittering façade of neon, is the downtown area of Las Vegas and birthplace of gambling. It has now, in an endeavour to alleviate economic decline, been transformed by The Jerde Partnership into a semi-enclosed urban mall. At the northern end of the the Strip you'll also find some of the older, landmark casinos: the Stardust and the Riviera, and classic motels such as La Concha. This is the best of several 'must-see' smaller buildings from the 50s and 60s that will doubtless soon be swept away to make way for new and larger development that as yet shows no sign of abating.

The Strip is a thrilling drive, but be prepared for terrible traffic – roadworks are constantly under way to accommodate the city's ceaseless expansion – and watch for hordes of wandering pedestrians who, enticed by the street spectacles, treat the linear, once purely car-oriented, Strip as an outdoor amusement park.

As Las Vegas is such a new town and has been thrown up so fast, it has paid scant attention to architectural quality. There is little to differentiate or to distinguish the building stock in the various off-Strip areas of town. Lacking a public domain, in the traditional sense, there are few significant civic buildings, and residential architecture is fairly uniform. Near the Strip and downtown are low-income two- and three-storey apartment buildings; away from the centre, families live in tracts of low-slung, pitched-roofed, single-family houses. Formerly built in concrete

Las Vegas: a guide to recent architecture

block, such buildings are now made of lightweight metal-stud framing. They are arranged in subdivisions dispersed over a grid subdivided into mile-long blocks. Wealthier communities tend to be built around golf-courses and behind walls (concealing some of the better custom homes), while low-income neighbourhoods are less likely to be gated. In recent years the gated, enclosed community has become the living environment of choice for the majority.

None the less, there are buildings worth seeing dotted about: a good number can be found in the south-east of the city. Just east of the Strip are the new Hard Rock Casino and Hotel and the bar, Drink, part of the trend to develop tourist destinations away from the Strip. And nearby is the University of Nevada at Las Vegas (UNLV), a young institution aspiring to respectability, which has sponsored several new buildings, including Holmes Sabatini Associates' (HSA) new Student Services Building.

South of UNLV is McCarron International Airport, bursting at the seams to accommodate the 20 million tourists now flying in each year, and about to receive a sleek new building by prominent local architects, Tate & Snyder. East of these complexes is the contemporary landmark of Michael Graves' neoclassical Flamingo Library, one of a city-wide group of architecturally ambitious new libraries built over the last ten years that has upped the ante for decent civic building in Las Vegas.

And there are older gems: the 1960s organic Las Vegas Country Club; the outlandish Liberace Museum in the grandly named mini-mall, the Liberace Plaza; and local governor and brain surgeon Lonny Hammargren's residence, a self-made, *ad hoc* assemblage of *objets trouvés* that is an inspired anomaly in a sea of more conventional custom housing.

Further south is Henderson, a new town founded in 1942 by the Defence Housing Corporation to house workers for the war effort. Here you can find Luxor-architect Veldon Simpson's own sub-Wrightian house, as well as the bright new offices of Tate & Snyder, a Barragán-inspired building that exemplifies the new sensitivity amongst local architects to considerations of locale and environment.

The next largest crop of interesting buildings is in the south-west portion of the city. There you can find the Rio, a lively example of the off-Strip, comfortably vulgar casinos that capture the local market. This one has to be seen for its magnificent neon pylon. Realised at a time when the sidewalk spectacle was starting to upstage the neon sign as billboard for a casino, the Rio sign is one of the few recent great neon artworks. Further west is a striking contemporary building, the new Department of Motor Vehicles (DMV) by HSA Architects. Its palette of metal, masonry and sculptural form is characteristic of much of the new architecture in Vegas. Local architects are drawing on sources such as Predock, Barragán and Rossi in an endeavour to find what HSA describe as 'an architecture of substance, which responds to the sincere beauty and climatic conditions of the desert where *faux* and cliché are the words of the day'.

In the north-western section, near the Strip, can be found such isolated modern monuments as DMJM's 1973 Las Vegas City Hall, and a contemporary landmark, the influential Las Vegas Library/Lied Discovery Children's Museum by Antoine Predock, the first and most prominent library/cultural centre constructed in the late 1980s to kick off the city's controversial library-building programme. However, around the corner from this rare display of public munificence (Las Vegans are typically hostile to paying taxes for public works) is evidence of the bleaker side of Las Vegas – a Paiute Native American settlement, established in 1912. The occupants of this 10-acre reservation live in mobile homes, and an important source of their income has been the discount smoke shop. This community, whose ancestors were amongst the earliest inhabitants of the region, will be moving to a 3700-acre reservation north of the city off US Highway 95. This move results from a settlement made by the US Government to compensate them for lands previously taken.

Much further north-west is Summerlin, the largest of the new dormitory communities, and a magnet for newcomers. Built on land owned by the Howard Hughes Corporation, Summerlin is one of the largest and most comprehensive of the new, enclosed and masterplanned, mixed-use communities. While its domestic architecture is predictably formulaic, it does include the Household Credit Card Service Center, a simple, bold commercial building built around an atrium by local JMA Architects.

To the east of the Strip, in the northern part of town, we've included just three buildings. The US Bank has been selected because, together with La Concha and City Hall, it is one of the city's few examples of high-art architecture from the 1950s and 60s . Another entry in this area is the Las Vegas Temple-Church of Jesus Christ of Latterday Saints, by Tate & Snyder. This Mormon Temple is one of the few non-casino buildings that can be seen all the way across the valley.

Mormons, who account for 15–20 per cent of the city's population, figure prominently in local history. Honest non-gamblers with business heads, they helped to finance the gambling industry in the 1940s, 50s and 60s, along with the mobs, local banks and teamsters. The largest sign-making company, Young Electric Sign Company (YESCO) is Mormon-owned, and Mormons were the care-providers of choice for the paranoid Howard Hughes when he invested heavily in Las Vegas in the 1960s.

Last but not least, we want to draw your attention to two landmarks outside Las Vegas that are definitely worth a visit. The first, if you drive in from California, is unavoidable. It is the crop of casinos at the California/Nevada stateline. The combination of florid Western styling, monorail and roller coaster that signals Whiskey Pete's, Buffalo Bill's and Primadonna resorts is an exuberant first taste of the unabashed amusement/gambling mecca to come. The second, way off to the east, near Boulder City, is the man-made triumph that allowed Las Vegas to happen. Built in 1935, the Hoover Dam initially provided not only the thousands of migrant workers that made nearby Vegas a viable resort, but also the billions of watts of electricity to fuel the neon and air-conditioning that have made it a seductive and habitable place.

Las Vegas: a guide to recent architecture

Las Vegas has been divided into six sections: the Strip and Downtown/ Freemont Street; North-east; North-west; South-east; South-west, and outside the city. Access to Las Vegas is via the Interstate 15; or if you arrive by air, at McCarron International Airport, signs take you directly onto Las Vegas Boulevard (the Strip). Although Las Vegas is relatively small, the buildings are widely dispersed and public transport is not an option. You could walk or catch a bus along the Strip, but this guide presupposes that you will take in the city by car.

Unless otherwise indicated, buildings are accessible during normal opening hours; casinos are open 24 hours.

The question of casino design credits is a complex one. The buildings have undergone many remodels and expansions since their inception, and many different professionals have contributed to their design. Furthermore, the architecture, sometimes utterly banal, has often taken a back seat to the interior or façade design; in some cases there is no record of the original architect. For these reasons it has sometimes been difficult to credit one individual or firm, or to find a date for the design. In such cases we have given a date for the completion of the original structure, although it may have been significantly altered since then. Where possible, a credit for the designer involved with the specific part of the casino we are recommending is also given.

Casinos in Las Vegas seem to change faster than the seasons; while the information provided was accurate at the time of writing, do not be surprised if some of the buildings have changed ownership, disappeared, expanded, or altered beyond recognition by the time you arrive.

There are many good Las Vegas guide and reference books. We would not leave home without Deke Castleman's upbeat *Las Vegas* (Compass American Guides); Alan Hess' historical study, *Viva Las Vegas* (Chronicle

Books); *Literary Las Vegas*, edited by Mike Tronnes (including writings by Hunter Thompson and Tom Wolfe), Henry Holt and Company; and *Learning from Las Vegas*, by Robert Venturi, Denise Scott Brown and Steven Izenour, MIT Press.

ACKNOWLEDGEMENTS
This book would simply have been impossible to produce without support from the following people: our friend Alan Hess, expert on popular architecture and author of the authoritative *Viva Las Vegas*, who generously shared his knowledge and painstakingly checked our copy; architect Arnie Stalk, indefatigable advocate of affordable housing in Las Vegas, who helped us get under the skin of the city; and the incomparable Eric Strain, architect and teacher, who took time out not only to introduce us to notable Las Vegas architecture, but also to review our text. For insightful conversations about the city, we must thank Las Vegas native George McCabe; gambling journalist Larry Grossman; artist Anthony Bondi; architect Joel Bergman; University of Nevada at Las Vegas (UNLV) architecture librarian Jean Brown; UNLV architecture student Sally Taraban; Las Vegas afficionados Eric Chavkin and Alison Pinsler; show designers Eddie and Eddie Michael Martinez, and Olio's Charlie White and Bob Bangham; and for giving us a bird's-eye view of Las Vegas, amateur pilot Gus Funnell. Last but not least, thanks to Tom and Jonathan at ellipsis for supporting the idea of the first guide to architecture in Las Vegas.

Las Vegas: a guide to recent architecture

Little Church of the West 20

The Luxor 22

Excalibur 26

New York New York 30

The Tropicana 32

MGM Grand Hotel, Casino and Theme Park 34

Monte Carlo 38

Holiday Inn Boardwalk Casino 40

Aladdin 42

Bally's Las Vegas, Balfy's Plaza 44

Caesars Palace 48

Barbary Coast 52

Flamingo Hilton 54

The Mirage 58

Treasure Island 64

The Strip and Downtown

Sands Hotel and Casino 68
Harrah's 70
Dive! Las Vegas 72
Stardust 74
La Concha Motel 78
The Gold Key Shops 80
Riviera 82
Westward Ho 84
Circus Circus 86
Stratosphere Tower 90
Boulevard Hotel, Bookmart, Steve's Buy and Sell Jewelry 94
Ferguson's Downtown Motel 96
Fremont Street Experience 98
Par-A-Dice Inn 106

Little Church of the West

We hate to disappoint you kitsch hounds, but the truth is that not all Las Vegas chapels are tacky. While the Las Vegas wedding chapel is often the object of ridicule and scorn, there is nothing garish about the Little Church of the West. Its scale, material, detailing and landscaping make it seem like a perfectly lovely place to get hitched.

Sitting next door to the Hacienda Hotel and Casino, the Little Church of the West, built in 1943, is the oldest extant wedding chapel in Vegas. It boasts the claim that 'more celebrities have been married here than any other place in the world'. Its nineteenth-century Western theming is typical of the theming of 1940s Las Vegas buildings.

The Little Church of the West was originally part of the Last Frontier Village, a Western theme park located next to the old Last Frontier Hotel and Casino. It was designed by Bill Moore, the architect and manager of the Last Frontier, as a half-scale reproduction of a gold rush era church in Columbia, California. The Last Frontier and theme park were torn down, but the church remained in its original location until the 1980s when it was moved to its present site. (It would be a good idea if more Las Vegas landmarks could be preserved in this manner rather than being bulldozed into oblivion. Having this kind of itsy-bitsy building alongside new monster casinos is what gives the Strip some of the same variety of scale and typology as the Sunset Strip.)

In case you do want to get hitched, a few tips from the omniscient Deke Castleman's Las Vegas guide: weddings are scheduled at most chapels on the half hour, so don't even think about loitering. And you'd better make reservations well in advance if you are planning on getting married on New Year's Eve – it's the most popular Vegas wedding date of all.

ADDRESS 3960 Las Vegas Boulevard South

Bill Moore 1943

The Luxor

If you thought your post-modern palettes could deal with any bizarre combination of deracinated cultural images – the blurring of simulacra and reality, of ancient and futuristic, of virtual, superficial and material – wait until you see the Luxor. This $375-million extravaganza, opened with a great fanfare in 1993, is already about to undergo a remodel, and a 1500–1800-room tower is planned for behind the pyramid. It was designed by veteran Las Vegas casino architect Veldon Simpson, who since seems to have gone into seclusion. The Luxor is a potentially great concept gone awry, a hodge-podge of Egyptian and other thematic elements that seems to be dogged by the curse of Tutankhamun.

Strategically positioned at the south end of the Strip, next to the 'medieval' Excalibur and opposite the MGM Grand, the Luxor is on first impression a sleek and dramatic building. It is a vast pyramid in black glass, with a gigantic replica of the Sphinx of Giza for an entrance and an obelisk in a lush landscaped garden. That water garden on either side of the sphinx with its regular bands of lawn and fountain is one of the most abstractly beautiful landscape designs anywhere in Las Vegas.

But at night-time – the right time in Las Vegas – the black glass means the building becomes invisible and the pyramid dematerialises, a trick that is fine for master illusionists Siegfried and Roy, but not for a casino. Its presence is signalled by the sphinx, by the laser lightshow that leaps around the garden and, from a distance, by the beam of light shooting into the sky from the pyramid's apex. The effect for visitors is quite magical, but not the one desired by the owners. Furthermore, the laser beam does not, in their estimation, shine brightly enough (it is supposed to be visible from as far away as Los Angeles), a problem which, short of suspending a reflective cloud layer above Las Vegas (which invariably has clear skies), is hard to resolve.

Veldon Simpson AIA Architect 1993

Veldon Simpson AIA Architect 1993

This dark and refreshingly understated edifice gives way to an interior of pure chaos. The potentially stunning pyramidal space, in which hotel rooms are seemingly suspended from the huge sloping walls, looks like an advertisement for gypsum board since all you see when you look up are miles and miles of harshly lit painted drywall balconies. Beneath the tiers of gypsum board the leftovers of several different theme-park concepts have been regurgitated, as though the designers didn't have enough faith in the strength of the Egyptian pyramid idea.

Competing for the attention of the largely youthful visitors is mini-Manhattan, an earnest, thrill-free ride on the river Nile, a high-tech simulator trip through the 'Secrets of the Luxor Pyramid' and a Theater of Time, which exits directly into Virtualand, where seemingly hundreds of little and grown-up boys play murder on Sega's prototypical interactive entertainment. The attractions are dispersed over a confusing array of different levels, created, it is rumoured, to accommodate some client-owned escalators that they wanted to reuse. The casino itself, buried below the ground level, is barely visible.

On the one hand detailing is shoddy, on the other pedantic, as evidenced in the desire for authenticity in King Tut's Tomb and Museum, whose accuracy was verified by Egyptologists. Symbolic reference to the treasure-filled tomb of 'Tut' is embodied in the lower-level casino, which is decorated in gold, red, blue and orange with reproduction Egyptian symbols, and features slot machines that accept $5 and $10 bills.

ADDRESS 3900 Las Vegas Boulevard South
OWNER Circus Circus Enterprises, Inc.
COST $375 million

Veldon Simpson AIA Architect 1993

Veldon Simpson AIA Architect 1993

Excalibur

American architecture critic Aaron Betsky probably summed up Excalibur best when he described it as the 'Toys 'R Us casino'. The primary colours of the conical roofs and the forest of turrets refer to the entertainment-industry tradition of the castle as repository of dream, romance and fairy tales, best exemplified by Sleeping Beauty's castle at Disneyland and the Neuschwanstein Palace of Mad King Ludwig of Bavaria (1868). The conical roofs, a collaboration between the Ad-Art sign company and the architects/builders Marnell Corrao Associates, employ signage technology, namely thermal-formed polycarbonate components, finished in gold.

Excalibur makes a knock-out first impression, especially when viewed from afar, thanks in large part to its brilliant colours and bright lighting. It is best seen from the intersection of Tropicana Road and Las Vegas Boulevard, which gives you a head-on view of the massive entrance pavilion. The placements of the turrets go a long way to taking the sting out of the big dumb boxes that are the necessary components, here as elsewhere, of Las Vegas hotel towers. Seen up close, the articulation at the top disappears. Equally weak is the access over a bridge from the Strip. Due to a lack of effective engagement with the lagoon it passes over – which a fully-committed theming approach would call for – the arrival is reduced to a universe of painted Dryvit. (Dryvit is an exterior cladding and insulation material of extruded, expanded polystyrene, reinforced by woven fibreglass. It can be used in swathes as insulation or moulded into ornamental shapes, giving designers a low-cost way to add dimensionality to a building. Dryvit is also the generic name for this category of materials.)

An hourly show features an 8-foot-high dragon who sallies forth from beneath the entrance causeway and shoots 20 feet of fiery breath into the

Veldon Simpson AIA Architect 1991

Veldon Simpson AIA Architect 1991

air. The interior of the casino makes a strong attempt at creating an interior world of its own by using bold rich decoration such as the chandeliers and the simulation of exterior stone walls that create the impression of an exterior space.

Because programmed tours are so important to Las Vegas, Excalibur has an entry court on the second storey for that purpose.

CLIENT Circus Circus Enterprises, Inc.
ARCHITECT Marnell Corrao Associates, Inc.
LIGHTSHOW Jeremy Railton & Associates
COST $290 million
AREA 500,000 square feet

Veldon Simpson AIA Architect 1991

Veldon Simpson AIA Architect 1991

New York New York

Why go to New York when you can see all its best bits compressed into a few blocks of sunny Las Vegas, with gambling as well? That's the thinking behind the aggressive marketing of New York New York, the forthcoming progeny of MGM Grand and Primadonna Resorts, Inc. The two companies have teamed up to create a $350-million, 2119-room hotel and casino complex that they hope will compete with the Disney-landish casino complexes now occupying much of the southern portion of the Strip. New York New York has a 300-foot-long Brooklyn Bridge, a 150-foot-tall replica of the Statue of Liberty, ten New York-styled hotel towers, a Central Park themed casino, and will be surrounded by a Coney Island roller coaster. New York New York's near neighbours are medieval England (Excalibur), ancient Egypt (the Luxor), and Hollywood (MGM Grand).

Its design, by David Downey, makes a nicely symmetrical layered stage set, with the Statue of Liberty marking the corner, Greenwich Village forming a streetscape, and the Chrysler, AT&T and Empire State supplying a tall backdrop.

New York New York may, however, prove an essential artefact. According to one devoutly Catholic Las Vegas taxi-driver we met, a comet is destined to come and wipe out the real New York by the year 2000.

ADDRESS 3790 Las Vegas Boulevard South
OWNERS Primadonna Resorts, Inc. and MGM Grand, Inc.
COST $350 million

Gaskin & Bezanski 1996

Gaskin & Bezanski 1996

The Strip and Downtown

The Tropicana

When the Tropicana first opened in 1957 it was a mile out in the desert, next to the Hacienda, the last casino at the southern end of the Strip. The Tropicana was heralded by a 60-foot-tall fountain in the shape of an art deco-like tulip. There were various degrees of mob control and influence in the Tropicana up until the 1970s; then, in 1979, it passed into corporate control when it was purchased by the Ramada hotel chain.

The Tropicana's presence on the corner of Tropicana and Las Vegas Boulevard is not what it could be, since the Tropicana as it stands is a mishmash of late-modern towers and nominal tropical theming. While great for framing views of Excalibur across the street, the Tropicana's Tiki idols are wasted. The space at the corner reads as residual rather than planned.

A high point of the Tropicana is the leaded-glass ceiling of the casino dome by interior designer Tony Devroude. It is billed as a copy of the the main dome of the Hyberian Bank building in San Francisco, which collapsed in the earthquake of 1906. The reproduction stained glass in the dome was manufactured by Judson Studios in Pasadena, California.

The Tropicana's other claim to fame is its 5-acre water park, installed by the new owners as part of an initial attempt to add themed- resort-park and amusement-park amenities to Las Vegas.

The Strip and Downtown

OWNER Aztar Corporation
ADDRESS 3801 Las Vegas Boulevard South

1957

1957

MGM Grand Hotel, Casino and Theme Park

Let's just get it off our chests right now – the MGM is a bloated billion-dollar monstrosity whose proportions, detailing and sequence of spaces bear no resemblance to anything that could possibly bring joy to anyone's heart. It's big and it's bad.

By the way, the Wizard of Oz forgot to give the MGM lion on the corner any real eyes. It looks more like Pity Kitty than the Lion King. In a town of lasers, showgirls, magicians and volcanoes, this is simply an unpardonable sin. Maybe the cheapskates who skimped on the lion will realise that business would improve if they installed a proper lion, with some teeth, sinews and flash in its eyes.

In order to get to the theme park, the MGM management callously forces you to go through the equivalent of two malls, which are basically indistinguishable from malls anywhere, and one hotel lobby. The 33-acre park, the first fully-fledged theme park in Las Vegas, is broken up into different areas such as Casablanca Plaza, Salem Waterfront and Tumbleweed Gulch.

The best thing about the MGM interior is the monster wall of video screens in the lobby and the silver, star-spangled metallicised hung ceiling found in the lower-floor public spaces.

The casino is divided into four areas: Emerald City, Hollywood, Monte Carlo and Sports. The most thoroughly themed is Emerald City, modelled on the classic film *The Wizard of Oz*. A 200-foot dome serves as backdrop for projected images in a special-effects laser show featuring lightning with thunder resounding overhead, the sun and the moon, a rainbow and a flying witch. Below are 25-foot-high emerald glass spires. If you really love the Oz stories then stay away from this second-rate recreation. (At the time of writing, it is rumoured that Emerald City may be moved.)

Veldon Simpson AIA Architect 1993

Veldon Simpson AIA Architect 1993

The MGM Grand is linked to Bally's by a mile-long elevated monorail designed by Gensler Associates Architects. They believe that the private monorail could create stimulus for a truly regional system, if the community accept its potential. They envision extending the line to the Stratosphere Tower and into downtown.

ADDRESS 3799 Las Vegas Boulevard South
OWNER MGM Grand Hotel, Inc.
THEME PARK CONSULTANT Duell Corporation
THEATRE CONSULTANT George Thomas Howard
COST $1 billion

Veldon Simpson AIA Architect 1993

Veldon Simpson AIA Architect 1993

Monte Carlo

Having succeeded in wiping out the relatively glamorous and sophisticated Las Vegas of yore, the casino owners who created a more family-oriented entertainment image are now busily trying to inject the old qualities back into the Strip, albeit in a more patronising and cute way.

Mirage Resorts is now about to commence construction of Bellagio, a $900-million adult-oriented luxury casino complex that draws its inspiration from an idealised late-nineteenth-century Tuscan gentry. Meanwhile, the Monte Carlo, another colossal resort project under way, is inspired by the Belle Epoque. Due to open in summer of 1996, the Monte Carlo is the product of a marriage between the self-proclaimed 'literal inventors of the mega-resort in Las Vegas', Mirage Resorts and Circus Circus Enterprises, Inc.

Located opposite the MGM Grand and to be connected by monorail to the Bellagio, preliminary sketches for the Monte Carlo show a *faux* neoclassical two-storey edifice, vaguely reminiscent of late-nineteenth-century Milan or Monte Carlo, complete with fountain and ornate cast-iron street lamps. This is placed against a backdrop of a standard 30-something-storey hotel, coated with an architectural icing on the penthouse storeys and dancing klieglights. The Monte Carlo will house a theatre built for headlining illusionist Lance Burton (illusionists are the most popular form of theatrical entertainment in Las Vegas at present), and its plush seats, balcony and proscenium are intended to evoke the vaudeville theatres of the Victorian era.

ADDRESS 3770 Las Vegas Boulevard South
OWNERS Mirage Resorts and Golden Strike (the development company of Circus Circus Enterprises, Inc.)
COST $325 million

Dougall Design Associates, Inc. 1996

Dougall Design Associates, Inc. 1996

Holiday Inn Boardwalk Casino

The Boardwalk is a classic American leisure-time environment, well beloved by show designer consultants for casinos and amusement parks. It was inevitable that Las Vegas would get an amusement-park-themed casino hotel.

The roller coaster on the casino façade is supposed to be a working model, ridden by mannequins. But in spite of the rides, the street-front presence of retail stores, and its well-executed amusement-park theme by conceptual designers EME Entertainment, the real thrills in Las Vegas are still going to be on the big roller coasters at Stateline and the sky-high roller coaster at Stratosphere Tower. Rather, the big contribution of the Holiday Inn Boardwalk Casino is its belly-up-to-the-bar aggressive stance to the Strip, along all 430 yards of its street frontage. Other casinos may be built up to the sidewalk, many even have major openings on to it, but this will be the first to actually use retail stores to entice people directly off the Strip, with no intervening landscape or casino area. It just shows that the rules in Vegas, such as they are, are always changing.

ADDRESS 3750 Las Vegas Boulevard South
OWNER Boardwalk Casino Inc.
INTERIORS Yates-Silverman, Inc.
CONCEPTUAL DESIGN EME Entertainment, Inc.

Fred Doriot 1995

The Strip and Downtown

Fred Doriot 1995

Aladdin

The Aladdin Hotel comes with full Las Vegas pedigree. First of all, it's already been themed twice – it started out life as the Tally-Ho Motel in 1963, complete with three-storey, low-rise, half-timbered motel wings, which as of this date are still there. After re-theming as the desert-inspired Aladdin in 1966, a new 15-storey-high Aladdin's lamp neon sign (part of which is now at the Boneyard, see page 162) stood out front, and a year later the casino was the scene of Elvis and Priscilla's marriage. During the 1970s the Aladdin came under investigation by Federal authorities as 'an R & R [Rest and Relaxation] center for the Underworld'. After the Gaming Control Board closed the Aladdin in 1979 it was briefly owned by a partnership that included perpetual Vegas lounge crooner Wayne Newton.

During its underworld days, prior to Wayne, the Aladdin was again transformed. Prolific Las Vegas architect Lee Linton designed the front tower with its ogee arches, and sign-designer Charles Barnard of Ad-Art conceived the *porte-cochère* with its yards of acrylic mirror-polished gold aluminum and moulded-fibreglass components. The *porte-cochère* still has that fresh Elvis-lathered-in-rhinestones, lights-reflected-off-shiny-limos glamour.

As glitz nostalgia hobbyists, we hope the management thinks twice before they re-theme the front. The Aladdin in its current version is classic Vegas.

ADDRESS 3667 Las Vegas Boulevard South
PRESENT OWNER Jack Summer

Lee Linton (casino façade) 1966–present

Lee Linton (casino façade) 1966–present

Bally's Las Vegas, Bally's Plaza

We don't think there is anything about the massing and scale of the Bally's Las Vegas towers to make these buildings the best thing that Los Angeles commercial modernist architect Martin Stern ever did in his long and productive career, which included his landmark southern California Ship's coffee shops. The towers were originally built as the MGM Grand for Kirk Kerkorian, who acquired the property in 1971, and were news then for their scale (big). Nowadays such size has come to be the rule rather than the exception with new development.

The low point in the history of this site occurred in 1980, the year the second tower was added. On 21 November the building was the site of the 'worst hotel disaster' ever in the history of Las Vegas, when a huge fire broke out killing 84 people and injuring another 700.

The show in the refurbished hotel, revamped under Bally's new ownership in 1985, takes place in the Bally's Plaza, facing the Strip. It is a choreographed combination of light, water, landscape and movement, designed to draw pedestrians off the sidewalks and through the casino. For many visitors it is part of a colourful journey that takes them through the MGM and on to the monorail link between Bally's and the current MGM Grand Hotel (see page 34).

The Bally's Plaza consists of a tube, surrounded by giant neon hula hoops, dividing a grove of palm trees artfully landscaped by Campbell & Campbell. As this tube meets the Strip, it dumps pedestrians between a grand row of what look like giant-size deodorant sticks or cosmetic packages lit from within. The selling point, the novelty factor and the 'show value' of Bally's Plaza are the changing colours – red, green, blue and white – of the neon and the lighted tube elements. The best thing about it is the scale – it's a big show in a town where big shows work well – and the ferocious integration of all the components working

Martin Stern Jr 1973; Friedmutter & Associates (new entry)

Martin Stern Jr 1973; Friedmutter & Associates (new entry)

together. It's not subtle and it's not meant to be. It's a good entry and a good exit. Like some other Vegas attractions, if you stick around too long it becomes somewhat less interesting than watching traffic. While its abstract quality makes Bally's Plaza different from other themed sidewalk attractions, it shares the quality of being most effective on first viewing.

ADDRESS 3645 Las Vegas Boulevard South
OWNER Bally Grand, Inc.
LIGHTING DESIGN John Levy
LANDSCAPE DESIGN Campbell & Campbell

Martin Stern Jr 1973; Friedmutter & Associates (new entry)

Martin Stern Jr 1973; Friedmutter & Associates (new entry)

Caesars Palace

In its current state, Caesars Palace embodies the best of all the golden eras of modern big-time Vegas. How can you not love a place where, at one time, you could literally ask the waitress to peel you a grape? And, better still, all funded by Jimmy Hoffa's Teamsters' Pension Fund. Although, by daylight, the casino hotel complex looks like a women's prison in Tehran, inside it is the ultimate Vegas casino – with low, dark velvet ceilings hung with crystal prisms that convert the interiors into an endless chandelier-like fantasia. Hotelman Jay Sarno's Caesars was, and is, in the best 1960s sense of the word, a camp masterpiece, a knowing parodic send-up of the impossibility of theming a modern hotel on ancient, classical lines. The irony is that, spiritually, of all the Vegas hotels, it is the one in which a real Roman of the BC vintage would feel at home.

A vast and majestic double drive, lined by Italian cypresses on either side of a long pool punctuated by fountains, leads to a lurid, pointy-eared, tiered *porte-cochère*. Designed by Marnell Corrao Associates (and now being redesigned as part of current expansion) with lighting and additional decor by YESCO, it seems to hover low – a pink-lit invader from Planet Tacky. A giant pulsating dome, like some colony of polystyrene insect larvae, houses the Omnimax Theater with its show recreating ancient Rome. *Three* people-movers transport you effortlessly into the casino (Caesars is so far back from the road that, with an ever-increasing number of pedestrians – 13 million in 1994 – the importance of luring them in has increased dramatically).

Don't forget to peek at the outsize presentation of Michelangelo's David – this one, unlike the original, is uncircumcised. The gold-plated cast-bronze, 4-ton Brahma in front of the hotel is a little trinket placed there by a Thai tycoon to ward off bad luck.

While the sweetest themed attraction is probably the floating Cleo-

1966–present

1966–present

patra's Barge, added in 1970, the biggest news on the themed-attraction front has to be the Caesars Forum shops. They mingle entertainment and shopping as effectively as has ever been done to date. A *trompe l'oeil* sky, with programmed lighting that simulates the transition from dawn to dusk, every hour on the hour, gives the shops their own atemporal place in time and space. Talking statues, created by EME Entertainment, Inc., function both as themed adornment and mechanical actors. Just in case you are under any illusion that this show has some real content – it hasn't. The point is showmanship – the pizzaz value of the statues getting up, prancing around and singing and dancing.

The down side to the Forum shops experience is the nasty and unconscionable death march that visitors are forced to take at the exit. While escape to the Strip, apparently free from Roman theming, beckons tantalisingly, armour-plated thugs herd you onto a non-functioning (on our visit) people-mover for a long, slow shuffle that forces you back through the casino in order to reach the street. But compelling you to prolong your casino visit is, of course, the goal of all right-thinking Vegas hotel owners.

Caesars Palace: PRESENT OWNER ITT
ORIGINAL ARCHITECT Melvin Grossman
INTERIOR DECOR Albers-Gruen Associates, San Francisco
LANDSCAPE DESIGN Huetting and Schrom
TOTAL AREA 85 acres; casino area: 117,500 square feet
Caesars Forum Shops: OWNER Simon & The Gordon Company
ARCHITECT Marnell Corrao Associates, Inc.
INTERIOR DESIGNERS Dougall Design Associates, Inc.
SIZE 200,000 square feet
COST $110 million

1966–present

Barbary Coast

The Barbary Coast successfully holds its own on the north-east corner of the big intersection of Flamingo Road at the Strip. Brian Leming's 1977 YESCO design for the corner employed a giant hourglass-shaped drum, banded at the waist. The corner siting of the drum effectively links the interior and exterior space, and the scale of the lights works brilliantly with the adjacent Flamingo sign. In 1995 four more storeys were scheduled to be added to the existing building, bringing it to a projected height of twelve storeys.

The Barbary Coast is owned by Coast Enterprises, Inc., whose largest shareholder is Michael Gaughan (son of veteran Vegas casino operator Jackie Gaughan, owner of Fremont Street's long-standing El Cortez). Coast Enterprises, Inc. is joining the theming game. They are currently building the Orleans at 4500 West Tropicana Avenue, styled after famous aspects of its namesake city. New Orleans has itself recently ventured into the gambling business in a big way. Designed by architect Leo A Daly, with interiors by prominent Las Vegas interior designers, Yates-Silverman, Inc., the Orleans is scheduled to open in December 1996.

ADDRESS 3595 Las Vegas Boulevard South
OWNER Michael Gaughan

Leo A Daly 1979–

Leo A Daly 1979–

Flamingo Hilton

This is the primal Vegas casino, in the eyes of the true romantic who has come to Vegas to see mobsters, hookers, flashing neon lights and 24-hour hipsters at play. The truth of the matter is that the Flamingo hotel of yore, started by legendary Hollywood playboy Billy Wilkerson and taken over by even more legendary mobster Benjamin 'Bugsy' Siegel (who was assassinated only six months after the opening of the hotel), is now history.

Only the fabulous, pulsating cerise and orange Flamingo signwork links the present complex to the mythological Las Vegas of the imagination. Oh, but what signage! Designed by Raul Rodriguez of sign-makers Heath and Company in 1976, it consists of *porte-cochère*, corner element, and a string of pink flamingos lining the fascia. And there is nary a more voluptuous and fleshy display of neon in all Las Vegas, no other that so truly defines volume by its unfolding flame-like petals and twinkling, undulating bursts of light.

Façades such as Rodriguez' inspired Tom Wolfe to declare: 'Such colors! All the new electrochemical pastels of the Florida littoral: tangerine, broiling magenta, livid pink, incarnadine, fuchsia, demure, Congo ruby, methyl green, viridian, aquamarine, phenosafranine, incandescent orange, scarlet-fever purple, cyanic blue, tesselated bronze, hospital-fruit-basket orange …'

Several generations of distinguished architects have also made their mark on the Flamingo, now Flamingo Hilton, including the ever so suave Douglas Honnold and George Vernon Russell during the 1940s, and Luckman and Pereira at their best in the 1950s, both distinguished Los Angeles firms. The Flamingo, as designed by Honnold and Russell in 1946, was the casino that brought the abstract play of California modernism to Vegas, upping the stylistic ante and introducing a new challenge of urbanity to the often rustic or more literal period-revival theming

Honnold and Russell 1946; signwork Heath and Company 1976

Honnold and Russell 1946; signwork Heath and Company 1976

that had characterised motels and casinos to date. However, the scale of their work was far too small to accommodate the demands of an ever-growing hotel casino, and all was swept away for the more pedestrian but larger complex that currently occupies the site.

The last piece of the original Flamingo was bulldozed in 1993.

ADDRESS 3555 Las Vegas Boulevard South
PRESENT OWNER Hilton Corporation
SIGNWORK Heath and Company

Honnold and Russell 1946; signwork Heath and Company 1976

Honnold and Russell 1946; signwork Heath and Company 1976

The Mirage

Las Vegas was, until recently, defined by extravagant neon signs that upstaged the relatively low-slung and low-key casino buildings they advertised. The town was also perceived as an 'adults only' venue, built on drinking, gambling, prostitution, marriage and divorce.

In recent years all that has changed, thanks in large part to the efforts of Steve Wynn, chairman of Mirage Resorts, who has been instrumental in transforming Las Vegas into a destination resort. He moved to Las Vegas in 1967 and acquired the Golden Nugget in 1972. He upgraded the Nugget and stripped it of its neon, rendering it the only neon-free casino on Fremont Street. Wynn is seen by many as the successor to two Las Vegas visionaries: Benjamin 'Bugsy' Siegel, creator of the Flamingo and the trend away from the ubiquitous Western-imagery towards Hollywood modern glamour, and Jay Sarno, who introduced the extravagantly-themed Caesars Palace in 1966, followed by the family-oriented Circus Circus in 1968 (see page 86).

Wynn has melded the panache of 'Bugsy' Siegel's 1940s- and 50s-era Vegas with the fantasy of Caesars and the mass appeal of Circus Circus. He has traded in the neon (which to him represents 'Old Las Vegas') for spectacle, and the easy glitz of the casinos built in the 1960s and 1970s for much more carefully wrought interior architecture. With help from a hand-picked team of architects, artists and show designers, Wynn is creating a series of high-quality themed casino resorts, of which the Mirage, a $650-million late modernist high-rise with tropical-resort theming in its site development and ground-floor public spaces, is the first.

The 'most successful property in the history of gaming and hospitality industries', the Mirage sparked a renaissance in Las Vegas, which by the 1980s had become a tawdry, jaded version of its former self. Wynn's hotel is the flagship of the resorts that now characterise the new Las Vegas.

1989

1989

A better class of brassiness identifies the Mirage (as it does the earlier Golden Nugget). The Y-plan international-style hotel is trimmed with horizontal bands of gilded fenestration ($540,000 of pure, vacuum-coated gold), sticking up into the sky like huge bars of white chocolate wrapped in gold paper. And there has been much effort expended in the lavish interior design by Roger Thomas of Atlandia Design. But it is the Las Vegas elements – the huge 20,000-gallon saltwater tank with its interior coral reef landscape, the flaming volcano outside, the 90-foot-tall glass-covered atrium with opulent streams, waterfalls, orchids, real flowers and plants mixed with artificial ones, and a computerised misting system – that are something to write home about. The atrium and the volcano, and the lush landscaping of the Mirage in general, help create an atmosphere of genuinely over-the-top zooty escapism – any theming the Tropicana ever tried as 'The Island of Las Vegas' pales by comparison.

The Mirage's volcano erupts every 15 minutes in a geyser of red-tinted steam and scarlet flames spreading across the boiling waters of the lagoon, to the delight of the hundreds of gaping men, women and children who pack the street. The assembled throng willingly risks death from passing cars whose drivers do not yet appreciate that the once car-oriented Strip is now, thanks to street-shows like this, a pedestrian hang-out.

The volcano is the first in a sequence of cleverly orchestrated, expensive attractions that prolong your arrival. By the time you've absorbed the tropical atrium, the exotic fish in the wall-sized aquarium behind the reception desk, and the white tigers of leading Las Vegas illusionists Siegfried and Roy which are languishing on white artificial rock behind glass in the entrance corridor, you've almost forgotten that you're being sucked into a casino.

Once in the casino proper, the dense foliage of the South Seas is replaced

1989

by a dense thicket of slot machines in a typically low-ceilinged, low-lit space.

Conspicuously absent from the Mirage is a wall of neon. The elaborate site development and themed attractions of the Mirage, like those of other new casinos such as the Luxor, make the role of signage in attracting visitors less important than it was in older casinos such as the Flamingo or the Stardust.

The Mirage does have a sign, however; it bears the 'first illuminated full-colour photographic pictorial' of Siegfried and Roy, and an electronic message display (similar to those in sports centres and now mushrooming in Las Vegas). Designed by veteran sign designer Charles Barnard of Ad-Art, with input from Wynn and design architect Joel Bergman, the sign is strategically located for maximum visibility at the curve in the Strip (so near to the lagoon that its installation complicated the structural engineering). It is a colossal but simple, uninteresting, gold and white structure that, significantly, defers to the architecture rather than making a statement in itself. Themed architecture is the new wave in Las Vegas, and the show designer has replaced the sign designer as its image-maker.

ADDRESS 3400 Las Vegas Boulevard South
OWNER Mirage Resorts
DESIGN ARCHITECT Joel Bergman (Atlandia Design)
PRODUCTION ARCHITECT Marnell Corrao Associates, Inc.
EXTERIOR CONCEPT The Jerde Partnership, Inc.
INTERIORS Henry Conversano
INTERIORS (guest rooms and spa) Roger Thomas (Atlandia Design)
COST $630 million

1989

1989

Treasure Island

The pirates always win at Las Vegas Treasure Island, a $450-million casino and entertainment complex created by the buccaneering, gambling and entertainment impresario Steve Wynn, on the same site as his own ground-breaking Mirage.

At Treasure Island Wynn went one step better than the traffic-stopping volcano at the Mirage, whose gob-struck street crowds have prompted urban critics to pronounce the pedestrianisation of the Strip. Here he entices punters into his apricot-coloured hotel complex with a street-side spectacle set in the Caribbean Sea. Every hour, the pirates aboard the Hispaniola and the crew of the British Frigate HMS Britannica duke it out in Buccaneer Bay until, amidst explosions, flying stunt men and cannon fire, the full-size frigate disappears underwater, to the whoops and cheers of the thronging audience.

Attention to detail characterises Steve Wynn's resorts. In the early concept stage, members of his design team dressed in full pirate regalia to get into the spirit of Treasure Island. And his hotel and casino exhibit an opulence and consistency of theme – from the gaudy, gold-bone chandeliers of Captain Morgan's Lounge/Registration Lobby to the Mutiny Bay Entertainment Center, from an 'ancient Moorish Castle' to the Treasure Island Buffet, Smuggling Cantina and Lookout Café.

Wynn knows where to spend his money to make money. The 'wow' factor at Treasure Island is the traffic-stopping Buccaneer Bay sea battle. The finely wrought eighteenth-century village nestling into the cliff face, the full-sized frigate and the lagoon into which it is submerged, and the hourly explosions and fires were all the result of a collaborative effort. Wynn's in-house architects Atlandia Design, worked with consultants The Jerde Partnership and show designers Olio Design, as well as an array of technical, pyrotechnic, theatrical and engineering experts.

1993

1993

Las Vegas city planners were initially baffled by Buccaneer Bay, as were cultural critics, not knowing how to categorise it. A spectacle rather than a sign, Buccaneer Bay represents the emergence of the show designers as the primary creators of meaning and iconography in Las Vegas. In defining the image of the city, they have taken up where the sign designers left off.

ADDRESS 3300 Las Vegas Boulevard South
OWNER Mirage Resorts
OWNER'S ARCHITECT Joel Bergman (Atlandia Design)
DESIGN ARCHITECT The Jerde Partnership, Inc.
CREATIVE CONSULTANT Olio Design
INTERIOR DESIGN Roger Thomas (Atlandia Design)
COST $450 million

1993

1993

Sands Hotel and Casino

The Sands Hotel is one of the best remaining examples of traditional Las Vegas glitz, although plans are afoot to build an addition with over 5000 rooms. Deke Castleman notes in *Las Vegas*, 'According to the (admittedly sensational) *Green Felt Jungle*, the Sands was controlled when it opened by more different mobs than any other casino in Las Vegas.' Frank Sinatra and Dean Martin were sold nine points apiece as an inducement to persuade their celebrity friends, such as Sammy Davis Jr, Milton Berle and Lena Horne, to frequent the place and perform there.

Sinatra continued to be a Sands habitué until 1967 when Howard Hughes bought the casino and cut off his credit, causing Sinatra to bolt to Caesars Palace.

The tube-shaped 16-storey tower, built in 1968 by Martin Stern Jr, has vertical bands of windows and a carousel arched top. It is the most lively and stylish tower from the days when modernism in Vegas still had some verve.

In 1978 the front façade and *porte-cochère* of the casino were remodelled to their present appearance – a series of circular canopies – by, respectively, Marnell Corrao Associates and Brian Leming for YESCO. Materials used were full-on Las Vegas glammy: prismatic polished-gold aluminum decking lit by red neon.

Of Wayne McAllister's original 1952 hotel, only the wings remain standing.

ADDRESS 3355 Las Vegas Boulevard South
OWNER Interface Corporation
NEON DESIGN YESCO

Wayne McAllister 1952; Marnell Corrao Associates 1978

Wayne McAllister 1952; Marnell Corrao Associates 1978

Harrah's

Casinos packaged as showboats, either floating on the water (as on the river Mississippi), or on dry land (as here on the Strip), are now a standard theme. They conjure up associations of the gay '90s – red plush and high jinks between mustachioed high rollers and gartered bar girls. But besides its associations with the history of gambling and hedonism in the US, the showboat itself, with its tall steam pipes, porches and curlicued Victorian trim, possesses innate charm.

At Harrah's Casino (formally Holiday Casino), architects Morris Brown and Associates, sign artists Sign Systems, Inc., and the Perini Building Company, remodelled the original 1960s building by architect Homer Rissman and Associates, pushing the boat to the edge of the pedestrian stream with an actual water-filled moat. Rigging and figures such as Huckleberry Finn and Tom Sawyer complete the showboat theming.

ADDRESS 3475 Las Vegas Boulevard South
CLIENT Harrah's
SIGNAGE AND FAÇADE Sign Systems, Inc.
CONSTRUCTION Perini Building Company

Morris Brown and Associates 1990

Morris Brown and Associates 1990

Dive! Las Vegas

Dive! is the brainchild of an all-star line-up of entertainment-industry big shots that includes Steven Spielberg, Jeffrey Katzenberg and Las Vegas' own Steve Wynn. The concept brings the total fantasy environment of the theme park into the shopping mall, both here at the Fashion Show Mall in Las Vegas and at the Century City Mall in Los Angeles. More outlets are planned.

The fun of Dive! is the integration of dining with the themed experience of a submarine dive, created by video screens, bubbling porthole windows and blasts of steam. On the exterior Dive! reads as the nose of a submarine poking through a wall of water. It goes without saying that submarine sandwiches are a menu item.

Dive! is an important example of a new national phenomenon: the inclusion of entertainment and themed venues as an 'absolute must' for any self-respecting shopping mall, and sometimes even as stand-alone venues within the urban fabric.

The Strip and Downtown

ADDRESS Fashion Show Mall, 3200 Las Vegas Boulevard
OWNERS Steven Spielberg, Jeffrey Katzenberg, Steve Wynn, The Levy Brothers
RESTAURANTS Skip Bronson
SIZE 16,000 square feet
COST $10–12 million

Meisel Associates Ltd 1995

Meisel Associates Ltd 1995

Stardust

All true romantics get Stardust in their eyes, and never get it out of their mind after one viewing of this classic freestanding sign, deservedly the most famous in Vegas.

The town wouldn't be the same without it. The sign flickers, it tickles, it cascades and it floats. The concept for the sign – a cloud of blue and magenta stars supported on twin pylons – came from Ad-Art's Paul Miller. When it was constructed, its 188-foot height earned it an entry in the *Guinness Book of Records* for the world's tallest sign. But note that the Stardust sign has already been tinkered with: the original pointy lettering has been replaced with snoozy old Helvetica. This, together with the fact that nothing lasts for ever in Las Vegas – not to mention the fact that the sign is nowhere to be found in the Stardust PR brochure – makes us fear for its life. Signs like the Stardust's make Vegas an international pilgrimage site for any aesthete worth his or her ocular nerves.

The long, low façade of the casino building, while lacking in finesse, still acts as an effective backdrop because of its sheer extent and dogged determination. The lighting of the hotel façade is a one-liner, a cosmetic diagonal applied to the late-modern banded façade of the 1991 tower block.

The Stardust was the biggest hotel to be built on the Strip during the 1950s. It was created for the low-end gambler by Tony Cornero, a businessman who had operated on both sides of the law. Cornero's business plan was built around $5-dollar-a-day rooms and customers with $5 a day to gamble. As Alan Hess has noted in *Viva Las Vegas*, the boxy two-storey buildings that housed 1000 motel rooms were lined up so rigidly and prosaically that they looked like boxcars. Construction began in 1955 but Cornero had a heart attack three years before the hotel opened, while he was shooting dice across Las Vegas Boulevard at the Desert Inn.

Jack Miller Associates (original building) 1958

Jack Miller Associates (original building) 1958

It wasn't until 1985 that the cloud of tainted business practices and mob influence that had hung over the casino was finally lifted for good – when the Stardust was purchased by the Boyd Gaming Corporation, owner of other casinos in the Las Vegas area.

ADDRESS 3000 Las Vegas Boulevard South
OWNER Boyd Gaming Corporation

Jack Miller Associates (original building) 1958

Jack Miller Associates (original building) 1958

La Concha Motel

We hope La Concha will still be there by the time this guidebook is published. This is just the kind of low-rise 1950s motel development on the Strip that gets yanked down to make way for new mega-resorts.

La Concha, commissioned by its present owners in 1961, was designed by Paul Williams, a prominent Los Angeles-based black architect with the most successful practice in southern California, designing a broad range of building types and styles, from the 20s to the 70s. The much-admired structure was seen at the time as revolutionary in Las Vegas. It is presently undergoing a remodel, but thankfully its exterior, at least, will remain intact. The thin folded shell *à la* Candela and Nervi was reinterpreted in re-bar (steel rod) formed around a wooden frame and then gunnited to create a vividly expressionist form.

The neighbouring Carousel Gift Shop, also circular in plan, was originally a bank and lobby for La Concha. It too was designed by Paul Williams, but has since undergone several remodels and changes of tenant. Along with the Gift Shop and the Pepper Mill, the low-slung, ranch-modern restaurant next door, La Concha forms a little bit of old Las Vegas. These buildings represent an era when buildings related more directly to the Strip, across an auto-oriented zone of parking lot and signage. This kind of experience is now so exotic that references to it are starting to reappear elsewhere in Las Vegas as a re-creation of the one kind of theming currently unavailable in the city – pre-1970s desert-resort Las Vegas glamour. (See the Hard Rock Casino and Hotel on page 130.)

ADDRESS 2955 Las Vegas Boulevard South
OWNERS The Doumani family

Paul Williams 1961

Paul Williams 1961

The Gold Key Shops

The Gold Key Shops are Las Vegas' sprightliest mini-mall in any architectural vocabulary. Designed by Berkeley-based architectural firm Elbasani & Logan, the concept is ingeniously simple: the horizontality of the mini-mall building type is exploited by stripes of silver and mint green cladding, punctuated by giant, battered, outward-leaning keystone forms that give the building a crenelated appearance. But these read as constructed forms, clipped on and modern rather than medieval. They function as the location for signs, thus integrating signage and architecture. Equally briskly detailed is the shade canopy – a steel-framed butterfly roof of corrugated metal – that fronts the building.

ADDRESS 3049 Las Vegas Boulevard South
CLIENT Kishner and Golden Investment Company
STRUCTURAL ENGINEER Martin & Peltyn, Inc.

Elbasani & Logan Architects 1991

Elbasani & Logan Architects 1991

Riviera

There is nothing more beautiful than the lighted façade of the Riviera Casino – definitely one of the high points of Western civilisation. The glass wall, designed by Federal Sign artist Marge Williams and hotel architect Nikita Zukov, transcends conventional categories of pop art, travelling directly to the synaptic receptors of colour and light in the brain, making them fire off electric impulses of pure pleasure. Emeralds, rubies, diamonds, sapphires, cake decoration, fine embroidery, cloisonné enamel – this is what the Riviera evokes. The medium is neon and scintillating light elements. At night, two rows of incandescent lights, located between the two-way glazing on the surface and a back surface of mirror, create an 'infinity lighting effect'.

The exterior of the Riviera turns into an eyesore during the day, but the interior casino is one of the most spacious and open in the city. It has had a chequered career: three months after it was built it went bankrupt and was taken over by the Chicago mob. Then Gus Greenbaum, the boss they had handpicked to run the Riviera, defected to the competition because 'he couldn't stay away from his old bad habits – the gambling, drugs and show girls', as Deke Castleman notes. As a result, 'Gus and his wife Bess had their throats slashed in a hit ordered from on high.'

The Rivera went belly-up for a second time during the big recession of 1983/84, before a renewed series of additions, in 1985, 1988 and 1990, made the casino the largest in the world.

ADDRESS 2901 Las Vegas Boulevard South
PRESENT OWNER Riviera Holding Company
ORIGINAL ARCHITECT Nikita Zukov
FAÇADE Federal Sign
SIZE 125,000 square feet

1955–1990

Westward Ho

The façade of the Westward Ho, remodelled in 1983 by Brian Leming of YESCO, is one of the ultimate art-director fantasies made real, because it does not refer indirectly to anything but itself.

The joy of the great Vegas signs, *portes-cochères* and casino façades and interiors was that, at their finest, they were a medium in their own right. In signs such as those at the Flamingo and the Stardust, the abstraction they employed, and their use of colour and light, created a milieu that was distinctively Las Vegas.

The only thing that in any way resembles the illuminated lightbulb, ornamented, vinyl umbrella canopies of the Westward Ho is the Westward Ho itself. (Oh, all right, maybe the open umbrellas of the Westward Ho look a little like a Ralph Steadman drawing of gargantuan egg-beaters.) At night these canopies become dripping fountains of light, their reflective ribbed columns shooting light up from the ground. At the same time light rolls down off the convex surfaces of the umbrellas, appearing ready to drop off on to the pavement in the form of the large bulbs that terminate each umbrella rib.

The Strip and Downtown

ADDRESS 2900 Las Vegas Boulevard South
REMODEL ARCHITECT Marnell Corrao Associates, Inc.
1983 FAÇADE YESCO

1961–present

The Strip and Downtown

1961–present

Circus Circus

Entrepreneurial *wunderkind* Steve Wynn, chairman of Mirage Resorts which owns, amongst others, the Mirage and Treasure Island casino/hotels (pages 58 and 64), is often credited with identifying the family market in Las Vegas and creating the themed casino and entertainment centre. But no one is quicker than Steve Wynn himself to credit Jay Sarno as the originator of that trend. Sarno introduced the complete themed experience to the Strip in 1966 with Caesars Palace, and followed up that success in 1968 with Circus Circus, a family-oriented casino complex at the north end of the Strip featuring a large tent in which live circus acts are performed above the heads of the people playing on slot machines.

Despite a shaky start – due to the fact that an over-confident Sarno imposed an entrance fee, unthinkable in casino culture – Circus Circus was an enormous success because it catered unequivocally to a mass-market audience. It went public in 1983 and is now owned by Circus Circus Enterprises, Inc., owners of the Luxor as well as several other casinos, both in Las Vegas and elsewhere.

Physically, Circus Circus has expanded into a vast, sprawling agglomeration of extensions, remodels and new buildings. Outside, it looks like something dreamt up by Archigram, the British techno/biomorphic pop architecture movement of the 1960s. A winding people-mover snakes through the project. Its colour palette is fuchsia-pink and white. Circus Circus is unmissable from a distance: its bulbous shiny 'circus tent' over the Grand Slam Canyon looks like a huge, metallic pink bosom – or maybe one of Madonna's bra-cups – complete with roseate nipple on top.

Inside is pure chaos, miles of typically low-ceilinged corridors and gambling halls jam-packed with people making their way to 'Slots-A-Fun', or the ticketed Grand Slam Adventure Dome amusement park, the Sky-rise tower or the RV (Recreational Vehicle) park.

Rissman & Rissman Associates 1968–present

Rissman & Rissman Associates 1968–present

Design-wise, the best thing about Circus Circus, apart from its brazen 'tent', is the Lucky the Clown sign. Designed and built by YESCO, the huge beaming figure, rendered in red, yellow, orange and white paint and neon, points gaily into the casino. Lucky joined other neon spectaculars in 1976, heralding the approach of the new era of family-oriented casino and entertainment centres. This imposing display – 84 tons in weight, 78 feet wide, 12 feet thick and 123 feet high – contains its supporting steelwork entirely within the clown figure. The marquee display board, measuring 41 feet by 50 feet, is cleverly incorporated into the design.

When describing the sign art, or indeed any other building endeavour in Las Vegas, beyond applauding the talented sign artists – in this case a team led by Brit Dan Edwards – it is hard to ignore the vital statistics. In this case, Lucky the Clown needs plenty of electric juice to power his 1232 fluorescent lamps, 14,498 incandescent bulbs and three-quarters of a mile of neon tubing, connected by 100,000 feet of electrical wiring.

ADDRESS 2880 Las Vegas Boulevard South
OWNER Circus Circus Enterprises, Inc.
SIGN YESCO

Rissman & Rissman Associates 1968–present

Rissman & Rissman Associates 1968–present

Stratosphere Tower

'High roller' used to refer to those prepared to gamble $5000 or more in a weekend in Vegas. Now it's the term being applied to the hair-raising roller coaster that zooms around the 'pod' 1000 feet above the Strip at the top of the latest entertainment attraction, the Stratosphere Tower. There aren't that many structures that literally aim this high. By virtue of sheer height, it attempts both to capture the imagination of tourists and create a new instant landmark on the skyline of Las Vegas.

The Stratosphere Tower, due to open in Spring 1996, is the brain-child of Bob Stupak, owner of the renowned downmarket Vegas World, who had long harboured a fantasy to build the tallest tower in world. Due to excessive wind loads, however, he had to settle for 1149 feet.

Construction of the tower (nicknamed 'Bob Stupid's Tower' by locals) has taken an unusually long time, for Vegas, and has been beleaguered with problems – there was a change of ownership part-way through (Stupak was badly hurt in a car accident) and at one point the structure mysteriously caught fire.

The Stratosphere Tower is now owned by Grand Casinos, Inc., with Stupak holding a 20 per cent share. In their role as owners of the Eiffel Tower of Las Vegas (OK, so maybe the open iron-work of Gustav's tower is a thousand times more graceful, but at least they are about the same height), Grand Casinos, Inc. can claim that their structure is the tallest tower west of the Mississippi, as well as 'America's tallest free-standing observation tower'.

The creators of the 139-storey-high tower have stopped at nothing to stimulate jaded palettes. The observation pod at the top of the tower features four wedding chapels, conference rooms, a revolving restaurant, a cocktail lounge and an observation deck. The roller coaster was orig-inally planned to extend out over the edge of the pod in order to suspend

Gary Nelson 1996

Gary Nelson 1996

thrill-seekers in thin air. To cap it all, the 'Big Shot', America's 'highest zero-gravity thrill ride', fires the bravest visitors 160 feet up into the sky at 45 miles per hour. A digital lightshow wraps around the legs of the tower in order to increase its already emphatic presence on the night-time Vegas skyline.

A new casino, restaurants, a retail and entertainment complex and a hotel are also being built at ground level in order to help the Stratosphere's owners recoup the $550-million construction bill, and plans have been announced to build a $40–60-million aquarium.

While other casino owners have opted for a fantasy-themed environment to draw an ever-expectant public, the Stratosphere Tower's attraction lies in its simple appeal to our fascination with the conquest of height and space. Its imagery is clunky retro sci-fi. We mused wistfully at how fantastic the tower could have been if Stupak had commissioned a high-tech architect like Richard Rogers, or a state-of-the-art engineer who combines art with technology such as T Y Linn, to design the tower.

Engineering note: extreme winds in Las Vegas meant that rigorous wind-tunnel tests had to be carried out before the structure was approved. The tower is built on Y-shaped foundations sunk only 12 feet into the ground. In an emergency, double-deck elevators rather than stairs would be used to shuttle people out.

ADDRESS 2000 Las Vegas Boulevard South
OWNER Grand Casinos, Inc.
CONSULTANT ARCHITECT Baldwin and Kranzlin
CONSULTANT ARCHITECT (pod) Cunningham Hamilton Quinter
STRUCTURAL ENGINEER Mendenhall Smith Inc.
COST $550 million

Gary Nelson 1996

Gary Nelson 1996

Boulevard Hotel, Bookmart, Steve's Buy and Sell Jewelry

If modern-day Las Vegas is a siren to worshippers of pop architecture, then she is a tease once they arrive in the city, since there is little commercial vernacular architecture with any real moxie. One of the few exceptions, albeit one not found in any Chamber of Commerce literature, is the pair of buildings located diagonally opposite each other on the section of Las Vegas Boulevard in between the Strip and downtown.

The Boulevard Hotel is blacked out with paint so that the gilt ornament – of a funereal Louis-Louis variety – is stapled on with a ruthless respect for purity of surface that would leave a colour-field painter breathless. Across the street a twin-bayed building, which in 1995 housed a bookstore and a pawn shop, has a façade composed, in breath-takingly minimalist fashion, of block screen pierced by circles. This lacy body of block continues across the space between Bookmart and Steve's Buy and Sell Jewelry, linking both halves of the building. Joe's E-Z Bail Bonds next door takes a similar vernacular tack with a different material. It employs lattice, that ever-popular American decorative standby, rather than concrete block to form a screen.

This entry is included only for those who have the strongest appetite and stomach for the startling juxtapositions of forms and materials found in real hardcore commercial vernacular.

Boulevard Hotel: ADDRESS 525 Las Vegas Boulevard South
OWNER Boulevard Development
DATE OF CONSTRUCTION 1954, remodelled 1992
REMODEL DESIGNER Nanette Da Silva
Bookmart/Steve's Buy and Sell Jewelery:
ADDRESS 512 and 510 Las Vegas Boulevard

Ferguson's Downtown Motel

Ferguson's Downtown Motel sums up much of the history of the motel building type in Las Vegas since it combines two favourite eras: Spanish colonial and the international-style/coffee-shop modern of Los Angeles. (We agree with historian Alan Hess that the credit always given to Miami as an architectural influence is completely off-base since most of Las Vegas' glamour was created by Los Angeles-based firms such as Martin Stern, and Honnold and Russell.)

The original motel wings are constructed of concrete block and have steel casement windows. The winsome octagonal turrets of the Spanish colonial revival building are capped with elongated spikes.

The high point of the new section of the motel is a simply-detailed flat-roofed motel-modern wing next to the street-side pool.

An additional attraction of the Boulevard Motel is that you actually drive through the old one-storey wing in order to get to the newer, no-nonsense wing at the rear.

The Strip and Downtown

ADDRESS 1028 East Fremont Street
CLIENT Larry Ferguson

Tom and Albert Franklin 1947 (addition 1956)

Tom and Albert Franklin 1947 (addition 1956)

Fremont Street Experience

Fremont Street is Las Vegas' downtown and location of its first gambling establishments. The area was incorporated into the city in 1905 and its first casino, the Northern Club, opened at 15 East Fremont Street in 1931, following the legalisation of gambling in Nevada. Fremont Street went on to become the most famous avenue of neon in the world. It is home to the infamous Binion's Horseshoe (owned by father-and-son operation Jack and Benny Binion, and famous for its showcase of $1-million bills, record-breaking wagers and the world poker tournament), Steve Wynn's Golden Nugget, and Jackie Gaughan's resilient Mexican-styled El Cortez (which shows a healthy resistance to the current mania for upgrading and theming, and whose unadorned, smoke-filled, nicotine-stained interior, is always jam-packed with locals who come to play for the lowest odds in town).

Fremont Street was the canvas on which the largely anonymous designers from prominent local sign-making companies such as Ad-Art and Young Electric Sign Company (YESCO) honed their art and left their marks of genius. Those marks were often transitory since Fremont Street is the epitome of a consumerist environment that thrives on novelty and change. Some of their handiwork remains – Vegas Vic, Vegas Vickie and Glitter Gulch – while much has now vanished, including the absolutely fabulous vibrating pink Mint, a 50s classic.

But in recent years Fremont Street and the surrounding area have descended into economic decline and urban degeneration, as have many other big city main streets in the US – Hollywood Boulevard in Los Angeles for one. By the early 90s, Fremont Street had lost a large chunk of its customer base to the more family-oriented Strip, and had become a tawdry, crime-ridden neighbourhood, passed through by tourists by day and frequented largely by the homeless and die-hard gamblers.

The Strip and Downtown

The Jerde Partnership, Inc. 1995

The Strip and Downtown

The Jerde Partnership, Inc. 1995

Furthermore, Fremont Street is in the City of Las Vegas while the Strip is in the County. Its tax revenues are a vital source of income to the City. In a bid to stop the rot of downtown Las Vegas, a consortium of casino operators entered into a public/private downtown revitalisation enterprise. They considered numerous schemes – including Steve Wynn's wonderfully mad notion of turning Fremont Street into a canal and transforming it into a latter-day, neon Venice – before finally agreeing on a project which involved roofing over Fremont Street, enshrining the casinos and transforming the area into a giant, controlled, pedestrianised urban-entertainment experience.

The Fremont Street Experience exhibits two traits that qualify as cardinal virtues in Las Vegas. One is sheer record-setting bigness, and the other is sensory overload. It was conceived by none other than the self-described 'place-maker', Jon Jerde of The Jerde Partnership, whose themed shopping and entertainment environments (including Horton Plaza in San Diego and Citywalk in Los Angeles) have had stunning economic success.

The Fremont Street Experience consists of a 90-foot- high space-frame 'celestial vault' which covers four blocks (1386 square feet/4.03 acres), and carries a Sky Parade and a digitised 'light spectacular' designed by lighting luminary Jeremy Railton & Associates and fabricated by YESCO. It transforms the street into a 'foyer' for the Fremont Street casinos which, collectively, now have more gaming facilities and hotel rooms than any one casino on the Strip.

Down on the ground, the newly-enclosed space competes for attention with street performers, kiosks, cafés, spectacles and the other attributes employed by the designers of American urban entertainment centres to counterfeit traditional urban street life. While it appears to have many

The Jerde Partnership, Inc. 1995

The Jerde Partnership, Inc. 1995

of the characteristics of the themed casinos on the Strip, with which it is in competition, the Fremont Street Experience aims to become 'the place where grown-ups come to play', rather than a family attraction.

The strategy of the Fremont Street Experience is to unify the existing neon and blinking lights into a single mega-attraction with the same power as a theme park. Aficionados of Fremont Street, concerned that it is to be museumified within its celestial container, feel that this strategy would compete with rather than complement the street's fabulous cascade of neon. Instead of being set off by the dark night sky, as at present, it would be subsumed into a blanket of light.

Though we're heartsick that Glitter Gulch isn't still open to the sky, we're impressed by the success the 'Experience' has had in drawing visitors; and the brief, hourly light show is spectacular.

But even the most committed preservationists acknowledge that the Experience is a dramatic concept that might alleviate the degeneration of downtown, and it might even serve as a catalyst for a comprehensive revitalisation of the area. Las Vegas is, after all, the epitome of the ever-changing hyper-consumerist environment where nothing lasts very long. Neon lights without economically viable casinos would not have much meaning.

The irony of Fremont Street is that it had to be killed in order to be saved. The Fremont Street Experience represents the adaptation of a suburban model – the sanitised shopping mall – to an urban situation, and project organisers are now endeavouring to use proximity to the Experience to woo prestigious retailers into the area.

Yet unlike the suburban model, which sprouts forth from virgin territory, the Fremont Street Experience involved the purging of the area through a vigilant public safety and clean-up campaign, and the appro-

The Strip and Downtown

The Jerde Partnership, Inc. 1995

priation of surrounding land through eminent domain (compulsory purchase), giving locals one month to vacate their residences. While the Fremont Street Company claims to be supporting the provision of affordable housing, the future of transplanted low-income families and the homeless is uncertain. The Fremont Street Experience is a stunning example of the chutzpah and optimism, as well as the cruel, raw capitalism, that have made Las Vegas.

CLIENT City of Las Vegas Downtown
Redevelopment Agency
LIGHTING DESIGN Jeremy Railton & Associates
COST $70 million

The Jerde Partnership, Inc. 1995

The Jerde Partnership, Inc. 1995

Par-A-Dice Inn

The Par-A-Dice Inn is one of the best examples in the style of the early Western-themed motels such as the 1941 El Rancho Vegas Motel. Western theming was much more common in Las Vegas prior to the advent of modernism in the 1950s. There is something about the horizontal lines of a single-storey motel that makes the motifs of ranch architecture (equally horizontal) seem appropriate, especially in what was once the wide-open desert setting of Las Vegas. You may not be wearing cowboy boots dusted with the red dirt of a ranch when you walk in, but that is the fantasy that this kind of motel conjures up.

Here the delightfully scaled tower fronting on Fremont Street is patterned after the water-tower buildings seen on ranches. It plays a flagship role for the motel and is not unlike the tower that San Francisco architect William Wurster incorporated in his 1927 Gregory Ranch House in Santa Cruz County, California. Although Wurster's high-art version is a far more consistently conceived and thoroughly executed work of architecture, the Par-A-Dice, a prominently sited commercial landmark, derives much of its vitality from the romance of the Western theming that its tower so effectively communicates.

We have included the Par-A-Dice because it represents to us a spiritual ancestor to later Las Vegas icons, such as the Luxor Pyramid or the many-turreted Excalibur.

ADDRESS 2217 Fremont Street

South-east Las Vegas

Vanity Park 110
Las Vegas Country Club 112
Regency Towers 114
Hilton Country Club 116
The Flower Peddler 118
Lonny Hammargren House 120
Clark County Library and Performing Arts Center 122
Student Services Building, University of Nevada, Las Vegas 124
University of Nevada, Las Vegas, College of Architecture – Phase 1 126
The Hard Rock Casino and Hotel 130
Drink … and Eat Too! 132
Liberace Museum 136
Satellite D Project, McCarron International Airport 140
Veldon Simpson's House 142
First Security Bank 144
Tate & Snyder Offices 146
Whitney Library 150
Sam's Town 152

Vanity Park

'Oh vanity, thy name is hairdressing', this building seems to say. It could easily have appeared as one of the sets on the 1980s American TV show *Designing Women*, as the kind of frilly beauty parlour where a character might go to get her locks clipped and blasted with hairspray. Victorian revival doodads sprout from every surface of the Vanity Park building, which appears to have started out in life as a clapboarded house.

It is very easy to envision the designer of the place standing back as the decoration of the building progressed, adjusting this and that little scrap of wrought iron, signage or painted decoration.

This is obviously supposed to be a version of the Wild West for the Little Lady – a more unusual version of the genre since the Old West is usually supposed to represent untrammelled masculine independence and toughness. It is also unusual in that this building comes closer to reading as a themed Wild West house in a suburban context, because of the residentially-zoned neighbourhood behind it. (Wild West theming is usually confined to casinos, and commercial buildings on arterial boulevards.)

In addition, Vanity Park is one of the few places in Las Vegas where you can see evidence of an individual who has really cut loose and expressed herself by applying ornament and decoration to an existing structure, outside the rules of both high-art architecture and the formulas of commercial vernacular architecture.

ADDRESS 1200 South Maryland Parkway

Las Vegas Country Club

There just aren't that many buildings from the golden era of exuberant modern expressionism in Las Vegas that are not now locked up behind the walls of gated developments.

This members-only sports club started life as the Las Vegas International Country Club and is now owned by the membership. It is presently undergoing a remodel, which we hope will not destroy the original form. Built in 1967, this is a small but exciting example of post-World War II organic American expressionism, in which structure, architecture and locale are completely integrated.

Feast your eyes on the radiating glue-lam beams. Marvel at the conical straw-hat-like roofs and the thrust of the *porte-cochère* a go-go.

ADDRESS 3000 Joe Brown Drive

Julius Gabriele AIA & Associates 1967

Julius Gabriele AIA & Associates 1967

Regency Towers

Built in 1973, the Regency remains Las Vegas' only luxury high-rise condominum. The top storey of the 29-floor 218-unit building is taken up with double-height penthouses, each with its own 15- by 25-foot pool surrounded by a generous terrace. If this isn't Tower in the Park juxta-position of urbanity to landscape, then we don't know what is.

The Regency is located in the grounds of the private Las Vegas Club, so you probaby won't be seeing it up close unless you are wielding a nine-iron. We far preferred this international-style mirage crowned with an intriguingly modified set of townhouses to any of the more accessible hotel towers we saw during our visits in 1995.

You'd think there'd be more of these swanky condo towers lording it over the Las Vegas skyline. But while it may be OK to stick visitors in tall buildings, most natives don't want to be cooped up in a condo. They feel more comfortable in a house or, at the very least, a low-rise condo.

The fascinating thing about the Regency is the tension between the late modern gloss of its styling and the changes made by individual condo owners, and modifications to the townhouses that emphasise the hetero-geneity of the building's pieces. From the east the contrast between the top floors and the shaft of the building makes it look a little like one of those gift cacti where a different species has been grafted on the top for curiosity value. But none of the disparities is so great that it overwhelms the original concept of the Regency as a modernist dreamboat.

ADDRESS 3111 Bel-Air Drive
CLIENT Paul Chanin
STRUCTURAL ENGINEER Joseph Zelner
SIZE 525,000 square feet; garage 110,000 square feet COST $11 million
ACCESS none

Rissman & Rissman Associates 1973

Rissman & Rissman Associates 1973

Hilton Country Club

This vibrant remodel of the 1960s Sahara Club is situated in an older residential neighbourhood, around the verdant, cooling greens of a large golf-course. Project architect Mark Lemoine has drawn on the vivid colours and bold, simple planes of Luis Barragán (who, with Antoine Predock, is a much-quoted source in contemporary Las Vegas architecture which seeks a desert vernacular) and Ricardo Legoretta (his Pershing Square project of 1993 in downtown Los Angeles) to breathe life and presence into a humdrum building. In a sense the Country Club remodel is just as much a landscape project as Legoretta's (or the designs of Barragán) since its real interest lies in the series of outdoor spaces it creates and its interaction with the surrounding landscape.

With a series of architectural devices Lemoine has turned arrival into a procession – through a square symbolic entrance springing from the perimeter wall into a courtyard in which a stepped red wall serves as a waterfall and a pointer; on towards the bright yellow, orthogonal tower, the entrance; and from there to the golf-course via an arcade. This addition to the side of the old shell gives residents external access under the shade of blue steel trellis. The desert landscaping – rocks and cacti planted by the brightly coloured walls – is a soothing counterpoint to the almost fluorescent green swards of the golf-course.

The one thing we would say to the new owners is that they really ought to remove the signage that now disfigures the project and replace it with something more sympathetic to the architecture of the Country Club.

CLIENT American Golf Corporation, Santa Monica
PRESENT OWNER Hilton Hotel
ADDRESS 1911 East Desert Inn Road
COST $600,000 SIZE 23,733 square feet

G C Wallace, Inc. (remodel) 1993

The Flower Peddler

The cheery, low-tech appearance of this blue-legged, lilac-fringed corner mall, located on a commercial pad on an intersection on the south-east side of town, belies its function: a large flower shop. Whereas contemporary casino designers go for literal representation of their theme, modern non-resort architects in Vegas, as elsewhere, opt for the abstract. This low-budget building – constructed for $55 per square foot – was commissioned by a couple who already operated a successful flower-selling business but wanted a new outlet which would also serve as a venue and expression of the wife's artistic and theatrical endeavours.

The young designers alleviated the drabness of a standard L-shaped, concrete-block corner mall with a curving, lilac, corrugated-steel fascia. Hanging low on the west side for solar protection and peeling away on the north side, it is held up by purple 'petal' supports on blue steel 'stems'. The petal motif is adapted to form shades over the windows on each of the masonry flanks.

ADDRESS 3525 East Flamingo Road
CLIENTS John and Liane Worlund
SIZE 5000 square feet

Carpenter Sellers Associates 1993

Carpenter Sellers Associates 1993

Lonny Hammargren House

Looking at the Lonny Hammargren House is the architectural equivalent of reading Hunter Thompson's *Fear and Loathing in Las Vegas* – an experience of watching someone go to extremes that leaves you feeling breathless, shocked, amused and engaged. Maverick Lonny Hammargren is a Las Vegas brain surgeon (who counts prominent boxers among his patients) and political figure. On his home, a collection of neighbouring houses joined together, Hammargren backs into the same territory explored by Frank Gehry, constructing different parts of the compound out of completely different materials. Spanish tiles and and domes are mixed with abandon, awnings vie with a giant TV dish for attention, artefacts symbolising technological advancement jostle with elements representing the past, such as a steam locomotive.

The Hammargren house is Las Vegas' best example of the one-off, owner-designed, personal fantasy environment in the tradition of Los Angeles' Watts Towers. It is the blythe disregard for rules that makes the place so fascinating to connoisseurs of the built environment – no one formally trained as an architect could ever bear to assemble such a wildly inchoate collage.

ADDRESS 4318 Ridgecrest
ACCESS none, but its exterior is best seen from Sandhill Road

Lonny Hammargren

Lonny Hammargren

Clark County Library and Performing Arts Center

The very first question that one has to ask about this building, popularly known as the Flamingo Library, is: 'what does it have to do with the town it is in, or with the desert landscape or its immediate context?' The answer is equally obvious. Nothing. What it has to do with is Michael Graves' œuvre as an artist, creating a certain kind of latter-day Le Doux/Boullée-like neoclassicism because he wants to. If that is the task at hand, if this is a form of plop art, then the question to ask is: 'how good a Michael Graves building is it?'

It is a handsome composition in a mannerist way, although its front façade says 'stay out, Culture with a capital C inside'. The library is stronger and more coherent in its exterior massing and composition than in its relatively straightforward interior detailing. However, the route from the parking lot to the auditorium seems at least as indirect and puzzling as the route through the average Las Vegas casino, and the ceiling of the auditorium is awkwardly interrupted by its ceiling beams.

In certain respects the Flamingo Library is a themed attraction, i.e. a traditional neoclassical temple of civically anointed culture in a town where such monuments are few and far between, built at a time when the town is just beginning to feel the need to legitimise itself by acquiring a mantle of culture, particularly if it comes with the guaranteed respectability of a name-brand designer label.

ADDRESS 1401 East Flamingo Road
CLIENT Clark County Library District
EXECUTIVE ARCHITECT JMA Architects
STRUCTURAL ENGINEER Martin & Peltyn, Inc.
SIZE 110,000 square feet

Michael Graves Architect 1994

Michael Graves Architect 1994

Student Services Building, University of Nevada, Las Vegas

UNLV is a wealthy university striving for academic stature and, even more importantly, sports prowess, in a culture where everything has a price-tag. The university is expanding rapidly to accommodate the burgeoning student population. New faculty buildings, including an architecture building (see page 126), are about to start construction. To meet the increased demand for a range of student services, the Donald W Reynolds Center was recently completed.

The student services building consists of two austere main volumes, linked by a more winsomely scaled and detailed barrel-vaulted lobby and lighthouse-like tower. The two wings, each funded by different donors, pivot from the central rotunda which, picked out in white stucco, highlights the vaulted entrance lobby of the building.

The arrival of a sponsor for the Jean Nidetech Women's Center created the need to add one more discrete section. A wall of sandy, square concrete panels slices through the chocolate-coloured concrete block at the rear of the Donald W Reynolds edifice, while the Newmont Mining wing – student development downstairs, counselling upstairs – is a collage of light ashlar concrete block that curves around a smooth, panelled inner volume. Inside, polished concrete floors, white-painted walls and exposed steel roof trusses create a serene atmosphere. The walls are clad with white, powder-coated corrugated-metal roofing panels and grey custom metalwork.

CLIENT University of Nevada, Las Vegas
SIZE 45,000 square feet

South-east Las Vegas

Holmes Sabatini Associates Architects, PC 1994

Holmes Sabatini Associates Architects, PC 1994

University of Nevada, Las Vegas, College of Architecture – Phase 1

Pure rationalism underlies the elegant competition-winning scheme by Los Angeles-based Barton Myers Associates for a new building for the architecture, construction management and planning school at the University of Nevada, Las Vegas, the first phase of which was scheduled to be completed in the autumn of 1996. Sadly, however, this scheme will not now be realised, having been shelved in favour of a less expensive design by local architects Swisher & Hall (formerly the associate architects on the project). We chose to include it none the less as we believe Barton Myers' proposed design would have been one of the most distinguished new buildings in town.

The architects drew inspiration from the cloistered courtyard environments that characterise other educational establishments, from medieval monasteries to the old universities of England and North America, as well as the vernacular climate-controlling courtyard buildings of the Mediterranean, Latin America and India.

Anchoring the south-east corner of the Las Vegas campus, the new school is an 'academic village' comprising, in its first phase, classrooms and studios, housed in two-storey perimeter wings and set up like small architectural offices; a library, contained in a round four-storey block in the northern quadrangle; and a two-storey, triangular administration building. The library and the administration buildings extend north and south from the central esplanade, a vaulted two-storey space that forms the main entrance to the school and houses a multi-purpose exhibition space and student-run café.

The buildings are intended to be didactic as well as contemplative, incorporating a variety of different structural, mechanical and cladding systems. They also explore ecological responsiveness by using – in tandem

Barton Myers Associates (unbuilt design) 1995

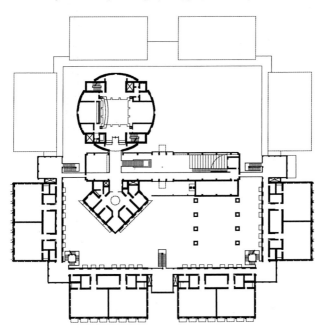

South-east Las Vegas

Barton Myers Associates (unbuilt design) 1995

with the courtyard plan – cooling towers, thermally inert massive perimeter walls and voltaic roof panels to achieve passive solar gain.

This design by Barton Myers Associates has two signal virtues. Firstly, it creates a large-scale order, with an opposition between its surrounding courtyard 'inhabitable wall' and the infill-like buildings inside. The design goes beyond the usual petting-zoo scale of most architectural projects to achieve a relationship between site and interior spaces that works on the scale of urban design. Secondly, the design could easily be built in stages over time, while appearing as a coherent design in each of its interim stages.

South-east Las Vegas

CLIENTS University of Nevada, Nevada Public Works Board
COST $8.3 million
SIZE Phase 1: 63,000 square feet

Barton Myers Associates (unbuilt design) 1995

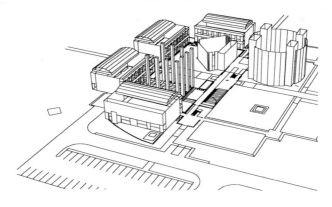

South-east Las Vegas

Barton Myers Associates (unbuilt design) 1995

The Hard Rock Casino and Hotel

Slick, knowing good taste that just can't stop winking at its coolness? Our verdict? Who needs good taste in Las Vegas? An advertisement for the Hard Rock smugly announces: 'Revenues from designated slot machines will be donated to organizations fighting to save the rain forests, including the Natural Resources Defense Council and Conservation International.' Does that mean that revenue from the undesignated slot machines goes to politically incorrect causes like men's rights? The copy continues: 'Guests at this socially conscious yet glamorous hotel facility will enjoy an environmentally clean and safe atmosphere with organic produce and vegetarian alternatives on all hotel restaurant menus.'

The Hard Rock Casino, with or without its embalmed exhibits of celebrity memorabilia and necrophilia, is so keyed down that it's like being in a Barnes & Noble bookstore (similar to Dillon's) with some slot machines and the music turned up. But that's not to say that the interior, with its lavish use of wood, isn't elegant and that there aren't some pieces of the place that we love. The gilded altar turned into a video bar (to be removed due to public outcry over its presumed sacrilegious qualities) is sheer genius in its juxtaposition of gothic spoils and TV technology

The Hard Rock sign in the form of a giant guitar is a great icon, plenty big enough to have impact in the vast parking lot and gigantic boulevard urban environment in which it sits. The façade of the hotel on the sexier poolside-elevation is a homage to the sweeping modern of Miami modern monuments such as Morris Lapidus' Fountainbleu Hotel.

ADDRESS 4475 Paradise Road
OWNER Peter Morton/Harvey's Casino
CASINO INTERIOR Warwick Stone, Hard Rock America
SIGN YESCO

Franklin D Israel Design Associates 1995

Franklin D Israel Design Associates 1995

Drink ... and Eat Too!

The best thing about Drink ... and Eat Too! is its sign. Designed by the client and fabricated by Ad-Art, it is a sweet, solitary five-petalled Krazy Daisy in polychromed neon atop a tall wavy stem adorned with rings of green neon and baby leaves. It perches on the corner of Harmon and Paradise Roads, brightening up what is a relatively dark corner of town (a residential neighbourhood) and distracting the attention of drivers from the huge neon guitar of the nearby Hard Rock Casino and Hotel (see page 130).

The next best thing about Drink, apart from the view on to the chic Marie Antoinette, a Rissman & Rissman-designed 60s apartment building opposite, is the exterior. The building itself is a set designer/cartoon version of pan-national neoprimitivism, with distressed bricks, chipped plaster, weeping mortar and muted colours on *ad hoc*, flat-roofed forms, like a version of a Tangiers *boite* that one might find on Los Angeles' Melrose Avenue.

Drink is the second of a chain of bar/nightclubs, following hot on the heels of the block-buster original which opened in Chicago in 1992. It is owned by Michael Morton (brother of Peter who owns the nearby Hard Rock Casino and Hotel) and Scott Degraff, who hit on the brilliant notion of making a theme out of drinking itself. Drink deliberately thumbs its nose at the prevailing health-consciousness and sobriety drives that characterise more straight-laced cities such as Los Angeles. The owners had rejected LA as a potential site for one of their nightspots, saying 'No one seems to have fun there.'

At Drink, the alcohol comes in a mind-boggling array of choices (50 brands of micro-brewed beers, 25 premium vodkas, etc.); it is never drunk from a mere glass but from mason jars, baby bottles and yard-glasses, and served up in a range of overblown bar settings. The Psychedelic and

South-east Las Vegas

Gerald Garapich & Associates 1995

Tribal Rooms, and the Main and VIP (featuring hand-rolled cigars) Rooms each consists of a mix of authentic and adapted thematic elements. In the Main Room, for example, there is a giant baby bottle, a kind of Drink mascot. George Nelson chairs and fluorescent blobs adorn the Psychedelic Room, and in the tribal Tribal Room frozen drinks are served in plastic buckets, hammocks hang between the columns and bar seats are fashioned from steel drums. The real theme of Drink is a robust, fun-lovin' relish of colour, light, texture and theme, and lighting effects so dazzling that they induce a state of intoxication on impact.

ADDRESS 200 East Harmon Avenue
OWNERS Michael Morton and Scott Degraff
SIGN Ad-Art

Gerald Garapich & Associates 1995

Gerald Garapich & Associates 1995

South-east Las Vegas

Liberace Museum

We have never seen a better example of the integration of art and daily life. The Liberace Museum is in fact so enmeshed in the fabric of everyday life that it occupies three entirely different storefronts in a nondescript late 1970s mini-mall where Liberace's restaurant (now Carlucci's) was located. This is not just a museum. Along with the Bone-yard, this is one of the final resting places, the *sanctum sanctorum*, for the gold-anodised aluminum soul of post World War II Las Vegas, before it was laundered by the corporate theme and family invasions of the 1960s.

The showmanship of Las Vegas is about the display of tricks, objects and effects. As the ever-popular American bumper sticker proclaims: 'The one who dies with most toys wins'. Nobody knew this better than Liberace. The toys are divided up by category: massive costumes suitable for the heads of Ruritanian monarchies in one wing, be-rhinestoned pianos and Rolls Royces in another, and personal memorabilia and china in yet another. The lesson to learn from Liberace is that trying is everything, that doing everything you can in the form of costuming, setting and staging to woo an audience will be rewarded, as it has been for other Las Vegas acts such as Siegfried and Roy.

A common element of many Las Vegas institutions – shows featuring plumes and showgirls, $52-a-seat spectacles like Cirque du Soleil, and the talking statues at the Caesars – is the creation of a spectacle whose surface supplements the often very genuine appeal of the show itself. This is particularly true of the lounge acts of individual entertainers such as Wayne Newton, the performer who has currently inherited the mantle of Liberace magic.

While you're continuing your intensive investigation of American celebrity worship don't forget to stop in at the Debbie Reynolds Museum

1989

1989

at Debbie's eponymous casino and hotel. The nice thing about this museum is that it also takes that Tristam Shandyish dilemma of integrating art and life into new dimensions: you can see the live Debbie Reynolds on display in the lounge act, mocking her own celebrity image.

South-east Las Vegas

ADDRESS Liberace Plaza, 1775 East Tropicana Avenue
OWNER Liberace Foundation

1989

Satellite D Project, McCarron International Airport

When we wrote this guide in 1995, Las Vegas McCarron International Airport, most of which was designed by airport specialists TRA, was typical of the massive, late-modern buildings that corporate firms all over America churned out during the 1970s and 80s. We have greater hopes for the new extension to the airport which is yet to come. Tate & Snyder have designed a satellite facility that will eventually add 52 new passenger gates and will double McCarron's current capacity of 27 million passengers per year.

Schematic images of the extension, by design architect Windom Kimsey, show a steel and glass terminal with a verve and lightness redolent of flight. We hope that Tate & Snyder will provide an articulation of detail and scale and co-ordination of materials and details, similar to that demonstrated in several of their other projects (see pages 146, 160, 184). This will help take the institutional edge off this now very institutional-feeling airport. Its exterior massing and fenestration show a lively articulation in the major elements, such as the popped-up-shed roof of the central hall, that will provide pleasing relief from the ponderousness of the original airport.

South-east Las Vegas

CLIENT Clark County Department of Aviation
AVIATION PLANNER AND ENGINEER Leo A Daly
COST $128 million
ACCESS from Interstate 15 or Paradise Road

Tate & Snyder Architects

South-east Las Vegas

Tate & Snyder Architects

Veldon Simpson's House

It's too bad that the MGM Casino designed by Veldon Simpson doesn't display more of the playfulness of his own house (located on the edge of Henderson in south-east Las Vegas). That said, it is indeed much easier to have lively articulation and composition in a small-building type such as a house than in a huge casino/hotel.

We're not sure just how Wright the Frank Lloyd references are, but they are clearly drawn from 1950s designs such as his Oasis project for the Arizona State Capitol.

Don't miss the next-door-neighbour which has a giant fanlight that looks like a down-turned jack-o'-lantern mouth.

These two buildings are among the few (outside the custom-designed gated communities built around golf-courses) to display the pop exuberance that you would expect to see everywhere in Las Vegas.

ADDRESS 6824 Tomyasu
ACCESS can be glimpsed from outside

Veldon Simpson AIA Architect

Veldon Simpson AIA Architect

First Security Bank

First Security Bank would be an asset to any auto-oriented suburban community. It is doubly so in Las Vegas, where unpretentious, small commercial buildings that effectively exploit their means of construction are few and far between.

Clerestory windows float above a stuccoed exterior with openings that read as cuts in the thick walls. The opposition of light, glass upper storey and heavy stucco is formally very effective. The thin roof of the upper storey gives a delightfully ephemeral sail-like quality. At the same time, the punched openings, the ground-storey awnings and the broad overhang on the clerestory windows, allow for control of sunlight.

This is the kind of Las Vegas building that seems to make the 30-year-old Venturi/Scott-Brown argument obsolete – it's neither a billboard nor a gratuitously configured duck but, rather, a perfectly well-considered response to its site, with a level of detailing and construction that could easily be achieved elsewhere in Las Vegas.

ADDRESS 701 North Valley Verde, Henderson

Swisher & Hall Ltd 1995

Swisher & Hall Ltd 1995

Tate & Snyder Offices

One of the practices that has breathed life into the Las Vegas architecture scene is Tate & Snyder, the largest architecture firm in the city as well as one of the oldest. Tate & Snyder has been revitalised in recent years and is presently working on several large commissions, including the expansion of McCarron International Airport (page 140), and it was responsible for such notable projects as the Sahara West Library and Museum (page 160), the Horizon High School (page 178), and this, its own office building.

It's a rare architectural firm in the 1990s that can afford to build its own offices, although many do of course remodel existing spaces. But in Nevada land is cheap, and architects, kept busy by the ceaseless boom, can afford to create their own base (it is said that there are more millionaire architects *per capita* in Las Vegas than anywhere else in the country).

Tate & Snyder has used the task of designing their own offices as an opportunity to experiment with environmental control concepts. Natural light pours in through floor-to-ceiling windows that are screened by a deep fin-shaped *brise-soleil*, while the temperature is controlled by a passive solar shading system.

This environmentally intelligent building is also chic, mixing the rough (exposed duct and truss work, corrugated-metal roof panelling, rocks and irregular stone walling) with the smooth (clean coats of iridescent paint on steel trusses, ductwork, ironmongery and plaster walls, a burnished-metal reception desk and light fixtures oozing urbane sophistication).

Designed by project architect Windom Kimsey, who was also responsible for the Horizon High School, Tate & Snyder's offices are built into a sloping site. Seen from the roadway below, the building is an eye-catching collage in hot reds and yellows. On entering, at the higher upper-

Tate & Snyder Architects 1994

Tate & Snyder Architects 1994

ground-level side of the site, one immediately gets a dramatic sense of height, light and spaciousness. The reception, administration and meeting rooms are on the mezzanine level, while the lower level is an open design studio.

There are so few good double-height modernist spaces in Las Vegas that the Tate & Snyder offices come as a welcome respite.

South-east Las Vegas

ADDRESS 709 Valley Verde Court, Henderson
CLIENT Tate & Snyder Architects

Tate & Snyder Architects 1994

South-east Las Vegas

Tate & Snyder Architects 1994

Whitney Library

Few would associate Las Vegas with literature – although there is much fine writing about it – yet libraries play an important role in the life of the city. They serve as cultural centres for a populace which feels that the compensation for an economy based on gambling is a decent education and library system.

Completed in June 1994, the Whitney Library is one of the seven new libraries commissioned by the Clark County Library District.

The centre consists of an adult reading library, a young persons' library and a 200-seat performing arts hall, all of which spin away into linear wings from the central, circular administrative area.

The north side of the centre is a blank, brightly coloured wall, canted to align with the commercial strip. Picked out in lilac and red, it is intended to attract attention without commercial signage. The south side is the main façade, accommodating the parking lot and entrance-way. A ceremonial blue arcade passes by the drought-tolerant landscaped garden on the right and leads up to the edifice of brightly painted, concrete-panelled, interlocking volumes. Yellow curving light-shafts are wedged into the reading area, providing articulation of form on the exterior and pleasant, natural light and useful niches on the interior.

Inside the centre, the bright colours of the exterior give way to a quieter palette of pale surfaces, carpeted reading spaces and polished concrete in the exhibition areas.

ADDRESS 5175 East Tropicana
CLIENT Clark County Library District

South-east Las Vegas

Holmes Sabatini Associates Architects, PC 1994

Sam's Town

Not all the casinos in Las Vegas are in the Downtown/Fremont Street core or along the Strip. But the casinos outside these areas, such as those along North Las Vegas Avenue above the freeway, and the Rio and Sam's Town, tend to have a higher percentage of locals who visit them to eat, enjoy the entertainment and gamble.

Six miles south-west of the Strip, Sam's Town is built around a 25,000-square-foot nine-storey atrium designed as an indoor nature park with roboticised animals and laser display. After listening to the clanging of the slot machines, noise-maddened gamblers who enter the atrium hoping to find a bit of peace will be assaulted by the amplified sounds of nature: 'a 16-channel, digital sound system connected to more than 100 speakers camouflaged among the trees and riverbeds. The sound of birds, crickets, frogs, wind and other forest chatter fills the park, creating a lively forest environment.'

Over the park is a pitched greenhouse roof and a courtyard. The walls of the hotel rooms facing on to this courtyard are decorated as a series of Victorian hotels.

The opposition of the large-scale, Victorian-style industrial glass gable to the fussy trim of the top storeys of Sam's Town is one of the better themed moments in Las Vegas.

ADDRESS 5111 Boulder Highway
OWNER Boyd Gaming Corporation

South-east Las Vegas

1979–

South-east Las Vegas

1979–

South-west Las Vegas

Statue of Liberty: Babe's Italian Ices 156
Nevada Power Company Administrative Headquarters 158
Sahara West Library and Museum 160
Boneyard 162
Rio Hotel and Casino 168
Department of Motor Vehicles, West Flamingo Office 172

Statue of Liberty: Babe's Italian Ices

The statue so nice they made it twice? 'Enough, already,' you're saying, 'been there, done that at New York New York.' But the deal here is: even though the new casino has the bigger Lady Liberty, this one was here first. The original statue was erected in 1886. This one was installed in 1981 as the mascot of this little shopping centre.

Tears came to our eyes when we saw the little Lady. They just don't make this kind of small roadside attraction in the shape of specific objects any more. In academic circles such an approach is known as programmatic architecture because the building usually reflects its programme in some way, becoming sculpture/iconographical marker. Exemplified by such landmarks as the Tail-o'-the Pup and the Brown Derby in Los Angeles, the heyday of this kind of architecture in the US was between World Wars I and II.

And yes, this time we'll bite and agree completely with Robert Venturi's classification of programmatic architecture: this is what he called a duck, if ever we've seen one. We're just worried that there aren't more imaginative clients and designers in Las Vegas with the guts to build pop mini-monuments with this much moxie.

ADDRESS Liberty Square, 4211 West Sahara
CLIENT Ned Gilbert
BUILDER Barry Houseal

Gene White (sculptor) 1981

Nevada Power Company Administrative Headquarters

This is definitely a contender for that macho, aggressive 'meanest SOB in the Las Vegas Valley' title. You could get a paper-cut on your cornea just by looking at the acute angle on the top storey, which is elevated on pilotis. The different pieces that compose the building, including the top storey, are unmediated in themselves and have no articulation – so everything appears as a kind of slightly cartoonish, superhero modernism. The same vocabulary works better on the interior because it is moderated by human activity and inhabitation surrounding a central courtyard.

CLIENT Nevada Power Company
ADDRESS 6226 West Sahara
STRUCTURAL ENGINEER Martin & Peltyn, Inc.
SIZE 278,000 square feet

Architecture By Five 1982

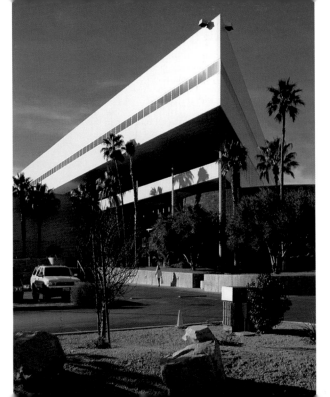

Sahara West Library and Museum

Meyer, Scherer & Rockcastle, in association with Tate & Snyder, have designed this library, one of the brightest spots from the recent brief era in Las Vegas when government was actually committed to supporting the fine art of architecture. The series of libraries of which this is a part (and which includes the libraries by Antoine Predock and Michael Graves) has produced the buildings with the highest level of design in the history of the city.

In fact there is so much architectural design in this building that we are a little scared. It's OK guys, we can tell from any one piece of this $15-million extravaganza that you can make objects. Let's see, at the last count the long half-cylinder form looked like Arquitectonica doing Cesar Pelli, the sweeping curves looked like Zaha Hadid, and then it looked like there was a little of that leftover Aldo Rossi influence that seems to be so prevalent in Las Vegas.

There's no way we were going to render a final verdict on such a rich and potentially wonderful stew since the building was still in the early stages of construction during our visits to Vegas. The programme combines a 10,000-square-foot museum with a 109,000-square-foot library, built around a visitors' atrium.

ADDRESS 9600 West Sahara
CLIENT Clark County Library District
EXECUTIVE ARCHITECT Tate & Snyder Architects
AREA 119,000 square feet

Meyer, Scherer & Rockcastle, Ltd 1996

Meyer, Scherer & Rockcastle, Ltd 1996

Boneyard

Despite the shift towards spectacles involving performance as a marketing strategy, Las Vegas continues to be defined in the public mind by its neon. Neon light was first discovered in England in the nineteenth century. In 1910 a neon-lit sign was created in Paris by Georges Claude, and around the same time neon was introduced into the West Coast of America and subsequently into Las Vegas. As gambling exploded after legalisation in 1931, Vegas went on to upstage other cities in exploiting the commercial potential of this pulsating, multi-coloured form of light.

Neon lighting derives its colour range from two forms of gas: neon for the reds and warm colours, and argon for the blues and cool colours. Its artistic effect depends on the type of gas, the colour of the glass and the colour of the powder coating on the inside of the tubes. The large signs used in Las Vegas comprise ornamental and informational components and consist of thousands of lightbulbs. They can cost many millions of dollars and utilise billions of watts of electricity.

In Las Vegas six sign-making companies have been responsible for the most prominent signs: Ad-Art Inc., Federal Sign, Heath and Company, Sign Systems, Inc., and the oldest and largest, the Mormon, family-owned Young Electric Sign Company (YESCO). Over the years these firms have been responsible for the most famous and influential neon-covered signs, pylons, fascias, entrance-ways and *portes-cochères* that frequently upstage the often nondescript buildings they stand in front of.

Commissions are won through competition, selected from design ideas presented to the client by several agencies, who function as designer, fabricator, or both. Sign-making is largely a collaborative effort. Its transitory commercial nature has kept the graphic artists – whom Tom Wolfe

established 1975

South-west Las Vegas

established 1975

referred to as 'the designer-sculptor geniuses of Las Vegas' – little known outside their trade. However, within the sign-making industry there are recognised masters of the art. These include YESCO's Charles Barnard, designer of Vegas Vickie; Marge Williams of Federal Sign, creator of the Riviera (see page 82); YESCO's Rudy Chrisotomo, designer of the Rio pylon (see page 168); Paul Rodriguez of Heath and Company, responsible for the Flamingo; YESCO's Dan Edwards, creator of Lucky the Clown (see page 86); YESCO's Jack Larsen Sr, maker of the Silver Slipper; Ad-Art's Paul Miller, designer of the 1967 Stardust pylon; and YESCO's Kermit Wayne, creator of such classics as the Mint and the Stardust façade.

According to Steve Weeks, a representative of YESCO, fabricating a neon sign is a skill that requires a 'time-honoured apprenticeship', and one that a computer can never replace.

However, while the craftsmanship may not become outmoded, neon itself is starting to find competition from new technologies such as computerised digital lighting, as featured in the spectaculars at the Fremont Street Experience (see page 98) which sign-making companies are being hired to fabricate.

As a result of this competition and the relentless remodelling of casinos, many of the classic signs are being torn down, and much of the unique commercial artistry of Las Vegas has already been destroyed. Local preservationists, led by YESCO, are trying to save these signs. A Neon Museum, touted as 'the final resting-place for old signs', is planned.

Until funding and a site are secured, old neon signs are maintained in the Boneyard, a large open lot behind the YESCO studio. Sadly not open to the public, this scrapyard regularly serves as a set for rock'n'roll videos and films. This comes as no surprise. The signs are densely packed, piled

established 1975

higgledy-piggledy on top of one another. They no longer pulsate with electricity and some of their light bulbs are missing. But despite their fallen grandeur, the Boneyard is an atmospheric treasure-trove of America's pop culture icons, among which can be found such marvels as the original Aladdin's Lamp and the Silver Slipper.

South-west Las Vegas

ADDRESS 5119 Cameron Street
OWNER Young Electric Sign Company (YESCO)
ACCESS none

established 1975

South-west Las Vegas

established 1975

Rio Hotel and Casino

The last of the great neon pylons can be seen at the Rio, a solitary hotel/casino complex located west of the Strip on West Flamingo Road, and much patronised by locals who come for the mix of good food and wine and the lively, unpretentious atmosphere that has put its owner Anthony A Marnell II on the map.

Anthony Marnell is an anomaly among architects anywhere. Architect, builder, wine connoisseur and casino operator, he is chairman of both the Rio Hotel and Casino, and Marnell Corrao Associates, Inc. The latter is the pre-eminent hotel builder responsible for the design and/or construction of a significant chunk of the Las Vegas resort district (much of Caesars Palace and the Forum Shops at Caesars, the Stardust, the Mirage, Treasure Island and Palace Station, among others). Marnell himself was the founder of the successful Rio casino.

At present the design fizz at the Rio is in the 'must-see' pylon, a dazzling cocktail of colour and light and zingy shapes that perfectly capture the flavour of its namesake. Designed by Rudy Crisostomo of YESCO, this is the regular winner of annual sign-design awards and seen by many as the finest contemporary example of a medium that is now on the wane. The top of the Rio sign is gorgeous, but the way in which it is jammed down hard on its big signboard is a great deal less appealing. The Rio sign is a swirling beckoning bouquet, like animated drapery, aptly summoning up a Vegas vision of Rio.

The hotel itself is a shining example of Las Vegas-style fast-track casino construction, about which there are many (apocryphal) tales. One such tale cites a firm that was asked to produce a working scheme for a new casino in 24 hours; another that Excalibur and the Luxor were reputedly built according to about nine drawings, just enough to get a permit.

The Rio has been expanded seven times, transformed from its original

Marnell Corrao Associates, Inc. 1990

Marnell Corrao Associates, Inc. 1990

one block, built in 1990, into a Y-plan high-rise with a cladding of fuchsia-pink and blue clip-on panels. It is now about to be dwarfed, however, by a new hotel on the same lot, this time a 44-storey tower.

Never has the late-modernist idea of curtain-wall cladding as packaging been more clearly evident than in the building type of the Las Vegas casino/hotel tower of the Rio and the façade of the Stardust Hotel (both by Marnell Corrao Associates). The freedom of the curtain wall to separate cladding from structure means that all sorts of liberties can be taken by changing the material of the cladding at any point on the façade, irrespective of whether that change forms an enormous fleur-de-lis, a giant Mickey Mouse or, in the case of the Rio, twin swooping catenary curves that seem to conjure up the (partially) thong-covered buttocks of the Rio's cocktail waitresses.

A new tower, to be completed in 1997, is a companion piece to the first thong tower, but with the motif reversed and applied to a building composed of a series of stepped, curving forms. There is also an additional central band of purple which resembles a large container of inexpensive, potent perfume. In both towers the charm of the Rio lies in its unstudied, cheerful Las Vegas vulgarity. This is an example of Las Vegas still untouched by overly complicated, manipulative theming strategies or elaborately plotted sophistication.

ADDRESS 3700 West Flamingo
CLIENT Rio Hotel and Casino, Inc.

Marnell Corrao Associates, Inc. 1990

Marnell Corrao Associates, Inc. 1990

Department of Motor Vehicles, West Flamingo Office

Despite the apparent pedestrianisation and urbanisation of the Strip, Las Vegas is still essentially a car-oriented and low-density area. It is a city of single-family, residential neighbourhoods dispersed across the desert plateau. Public transit cannot keep up with the population growth and the city's roads are in a constant state of rebuilding, with the result that traffic, particularly in the centre of town, is horrendous. It seems only fitting therefore that the local Department of Motor Vehicles should express its importance in such an attention-getting design.

The new DMV is located on an expanse of undeveloped land on the west side of town, which is masterplanned to incorporate an adjacent park. It provides a one-stop 'shop' for everything relating to the automobile: administration and public services, computer and data centre, physical inspection site, warehouse, distribution centre and conference rooms. Given the multiplicity of services, it is more a mall than a shop, and the designers did in fact base the organisation on a 'retail mall circulation pattern for on-site movement and a bank-queuing pattern for the public services areas'.

The resulting plan is a loose-knit arrangement of one- and two-storey articulated volumes embracing a fan-shaped plaza. The unifying element in the design is a continuous wall of two-tone concrete block (smooth and rough textured) that is a staple in contemporary Vegas architecture, and an overall palette of steel cladding and sand-coloured masonry solids that blend with the dry desert site.

Designed to reduce energy consumption by harnessing the sunlight – a novel concept for many builders in Las Vegas – the DMV makes stylistic references to the gas-guzzling device it represents. The aluminium clad-

Holmes Sabatini Associates Architects 1994

ding over the entranceway invokes engine grilles, the tapering steel columns on the Vehicle Registration Plaza seem to imply car jacks, and the form of the state of Nevada is incorporated into a bank of windows.

South-west Las Vegas

ADDRESS 8250 West Flamingo
CLIENT State of Nevada Department of Motor Vehicles and Public Safety
LANDSCAPE ARCHITECTS Zunino Associates

Holmes Sabatini Associates Architects 1994

Holmes Sabatini Associates Architects 1994

North-east Las Vegas

Horizon High School 178
US Bank 182
Las Vegas Temple-Church of Jesus Christ of Latter Day Saints 184

Horizon High School

The Horizon High School, designed by Windom Kimsey of Tate & Snyder, is a teaching and support centre for problem teenagers that is simultaneously responsive to its site, its climate and its programme.

The advent of air-conditioning has relieved designers of the need to deal efficiently with climate-control. It has enabled cities such as Las Vegas to be created in hostile environments. Indifference to the local ecology in this city invariably manifests itself both inside and outside. Much of Las Vegas' built environment is utterly devoid of shading devices. Trees, canopies and arcades do not adorn the various vast plateaux – parking lots, wide roads, shopping mall forecourts and so on – that one must traverse to get around Las Vegas. Most buildings in the city fight the desert. As a consequence, the Horizon High School is one of the few buildings in Las Vegas that actually responds to its desert site, by using the model of the courtyard building, and a high garden wall to provide shade and a sense of refuge and protection.

Visiting there on a 110-degree afternoon, we passed from a scorching car-park into a deliciously cool and shady courtyard. A high, curving perimeter wall creates a yard in the interstitial open space formed between the two school buildings. One houses administration, child-care and general activities in an oblong wing at the front of the site. The other, an L-shaped wing housing classrooms and laboratories, pivots from it. It opens on to a high corridor suffused with light from clerestory windows. The hardness of the corridor's exposed masonry walls and polished concrete floors is softened by a patterned floor design and a palette of warm reds and yellows.

Continuing the Las Vegas tradition of building in concrete block, Horizon High School is built out of masonry of variegated texture and hue, concrete and curved-steel roofing. Security and vandal-proofing

Tate & Snyder Architects 1993

Tate & Snyder Architects 1993

requirements have been given architectural forms that are assets rather than liabilities. Dense, high walls that provide welcome relief from the sun are given human scale in the textured and striped concrete-block walls, decoratively punctuated by glass block and rows of tiny windows. The outside courtyard, a smooth plane of scored concrete, is dotted with benches and palm trees in concrete planters.

North-east Las Vegas

ADDRESS 4560 West Harmon Avenue
PROJECT ARCHITECT Windom Kimsey
SIZE 31,816 square feet
COST $3,037,000

Tate & Snyder Architects 1993

North-east Las Vegas

Tate & Snyder Architects 1993

US Bank

Including the US Bank was a tough call. Frankly, guides to most major American cities wouldn't include such a building. It is on our roll-call simply because it is one of only a few extant examples of early attempts to produce high-art architecture in Las Vegas. We felt it was important to emphasise such remaining examples in order to put the current crop of new buildings with architectural merit in perspective.

Originally constructed for Frontier Savings, the building boasts a giant east-facing screen in the great Vegas and LA 1950s and 60s tradition of throwing up screens in front of blank walls to create dramatic patterning and shadows. The flat roof of the double-height New Formalism portico on Charleston is held aloft by impossibly spindly steel columns. There is some delightful period detailing at the US Bank, such as the extension of the *porte-cochère* roof as an overturning wall past the edge of the building, and a corner window in the north façade that articulates the west wall shooting past the building as an independently articulated element.

As long as you're on this corner, don't miss the wonderful professional building across the street at 721 Charleston. The exposed roof joists have wickedly tapered ends sandwiched between what look like twin 2 x 6 pilasters, with solid end-walls of block. It's a gem of a modernist building, whose architecture is created by its means of construction – a perfect example of the kind of building that makes up so much of Las Vegas yet is so little studied because of the feverish interest that the casino hotels of Fremont Street and the Strip hold for students of popular culture.

ADDRESS 801 East Charleston

Circa 1962

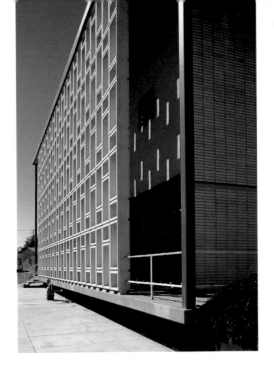

North-east Las Vegas

Circa 1962

Las Vegas Temple-Church of Jesus Christ of Latter Day Saints

There's no question that the Mormons are one of only a handful of religious denominations in the US that still knows how to throw up a really splashy place of worship. OK, we'll admit that the Scientologists have quite a trained eye for choice pieces of period-revival real estate, the Greek Orthodox for traditional replications, and the Sikhs for gold domes, but there is something about the white, crystalline, gilt-edged architecture of modern Mormon that puts it head and shoulders above the competition. And just what might that something be? Part of it, in the case of this Tate & Snyder design, is five gothicky spires staking down a finned, zig-zag moderne-tinged apse.

As well as being Wrightian in its prow-like form, the church also reminds us of the work of that madcap Californian eclectic, English-born Robert Stacy Judd – his First Baptist Church of 1928–32 in Ventura, California, for example.

With its gold angels glinting from on high, this is one of the few Las Vegas landmarks that is *not* a casino that you can read all the way across the valley. We pray that Tate & Snyder, in its role as Las Vegas' largest architecture firm, will keep a place in its repertoire for other work as eccentric and original as this movie-palace gothic temple.

ADDRESS 827 Temple View Drive
STRUCTURAL ENGINEER Martin & Peltyn, Inc.

Tate & Snyder Architects 1989

North-west Las Vegas

Las Vegas City Hall Complex 188
Las Vegas Library/Lied Discovery Children's Museum 190
Clark County Governmental Center 194
United Blood Services: Blood Donation Center 198
Siegfried and Roy's House 200
Household Credit Card Service Center 202

Las Vegas City Hall Complex

The Las Vegas City Hall complex is located at the northern end of Las Vegas Boulevard, and stands as a bastion of civic architectural presence in a downtown that, apart from the nearby neoclassical post office and a smattering of corporate offices, largely comprises undistinguished casino and hotel towers. It was built to accommodate the municipal needs of a fast-expanding population under one roof, and houses the city's administrative functions, police and fire departments and municipal courts.

The severely geometrical organisation of the project consists of a three-storey circular administrative building which intersects with a quadrant-shaped tower. The north side of the building, facing the courtyard, is composed of a curtain wall of bronze glass. An abstract sunburst design is displayed against the blank south-facing façade of the tower.

The building is a wonderful period-piece of 1960s modernist design considered as formal object. Experientially the courtyard is a barren space, with neither landscaping nor articulation to relieve its concrete harshness.

ADDRESS 400 Stewart Avenue
CLIENT City of Las Vegas
SIZE 270,000 square feet

North-west Las Vegas

DMJM Las Vegas 1973

DMJM Las Vegas 1973

Las Vegas Library/Lied Discovery Children's Museum

In Las Vegas, libraries have traditionally served as more than just repositories of books. They have also had a role as community centres and, in many cases, as sole institutional support and outlet for art and cultural activities.

In 1985, 15 years after the last library was built, director of Las Vegas Library District, Charles Hunsberger, initiated a visionary building programme of architecturally distinguished library/cultural centres. A bond measure was passed to finance seven such buildings and Antoine Predock's Las Vegas Library/Discovery Museum was the first to be built.

The building instantly became a symbol for public architecture in Las Vegas. But its very monumentality, together with the high profile of the other libraries that followed, engendered a hostile reaction from many members of the public. They took to heart claims by some local politicians that Hunsberger was 'frivolously spending [tax-payers'] money on wonderful pieces of architecture', and forced him out of office.

Perched on a promontory overlooking downtown from the north, Predock's Las Vegas Library/Discovery Museum is a miniature citadel of culture. It consists of a collection of distinct volumes – a sandstone prow containing the administration, a 112-foot-high science tower, a barrel-vaulted reading room with pyramidal skylight, and a conical pre–cast concrete party room. There is an equally heterogeneous array of openings – square and round windows, thin and fat ones, peepholes, triangular skylights, square grilles and arched doorways.

The drama of the building's exterior comes from the orchestration of these diverse components into a single sculptural whole. Its strong architectural presence and high standards of craftmanship raise levels of expectation for not only architecture in the city generally, but also for the

Antoine Predock Architect 1989

North-west Las Vegas

Antoine Predock Architect 1989

interior of the building itself. The latter, however, turns out to be a letdown. The successful collision of assorted forms on the exterior gives way to chaotic planning on the inside – functions squashed into unyielding spaces, over-complicated structure and unpalatable colour combinations. Internal courtyards are largely unused; the forecourt is unshaded, while the landscaping still seems like a work in progress. The original monumental line of palm trees bit the dust, as did a fountain spilling out of the screen-wall that stretches from the library to one side – the city's homeless were using it to bath in. A typically Las Vegan solution was to turn off the water (it functions now and then) rather than provide alternative bathing facilities.

Predock's Las Vegas Library/Discovery Museum is largely style over substance. It appears as if the budget has been spent on the public face rather than the public's comfort. But at least the building's public face has the exuberance and the formal panache to make a strong case for high-art architecture in a town that is just beginning to understand the power that architecture can possess.

North-west Las Vegas

ADDRESS 833 Las Vegas Boulevard North
LANDSCAPE DESIGN CONSULTANT Swisher & Hall Ltd
STRUCTURAL ENGINEER Martin & Peltyn, Inc.
SIZE 110,000 square feet

Antoine Predock Architect 1989

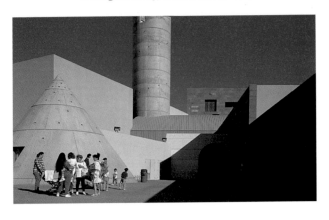

Antoine Predock Architect 1989

Clark County Governmental Center

Driving northwards on Interstate 15, the Clark County Governmental Center emerges into view behind a forest of towers. The low sculptural shape with its oddly flattened pyramid, curving, central rotunda and warm, red-textured stone presents a dramatic silhouette.

We stood in front of the Clark County Governmental Center marvelling to ourselves: 'I guess the Luxor casino wasn't enough – it's the pyramid so nice they've made it twice.' (And the joke so nice we've used it twice.) Here the pyramid is at a much dinkier scale than the one at the Luxor, and faced in sandstone rather than mirror glass.

Like the Luxor, the Clark County Governmental Center reads best from a distance: an expressionistic and sculptural opposition of curving main building façade, pyramid and colossal, freestanding pillars. Up close some of its detailing – the juxtaposition of the stucco ceiling of the colonnade to the sandstone cladding on the walls outside it, or the truly awkward proportions and fenestration of the colonnaded façade – is disappointing.

While casino architecture in Vegas does not generally relate to its desert location (apart from the romantic imagery of far-off sandy climes of the Sahara, the Dunes and the Luxor), contemporary non-casino architecture is rife with references to desert building, specifically that of near-neighbour, New Mexico. Following the example set in the Las Vegas Library and Discovery Museum (page 190) by Alberquerque-based Antoine Predock (who also competed for this project and who draws inspiration from the primitive building of New Mexico, if not its climate-control systems), architects have been seeking a more authentic regional language. They have taken the masonry construction that had become the tradition in Las Vegas – as a result of high winds and poor local craftsmanship – and adapted it into a building vocabulary of earthen forms:

C W Fentress J H Bradburn and Associates, PC 1985

North-west Las Vegas

C W Fentress J H Bradburn and Associates, PC 1985

pyramids (inverted, truncated, flattened); cones; tiny, square windows; smooth and textured sandstone; dry, desert landscaping of crushed stones, red rocks and cacti; and a sense of weight and presence.

This approach characterises the new Clark County Governmental Center, whose stepped sequence of seemingly earthen forms wrapped around a public amphitheatre, attempts to invoke the openness of government as well as the natural forms native to Nevada.

The building is rife with the kind of contradictions that characterise Las Vegas: as the open government centre is located at the intersection of the raised Interstate 15 freeway and the busy commercial West Charleston Boulevard, it is, for the main part, neither accessible nor visible to pedestrians; deciduous trees, not xeriscaped landscaping, fill the amphitheatre; and the terracotta sandstone exterior masks the inevitable steel frame and concrete core.

Whether or not our atavistic instincts are able to intuit the building's allusions to 'the remains of volcanic pyramids', prickly pears (in the network of clerestory lights protruding from the auditorium roof) and natural ceremonial passageways (in the entrances) – as claimed by its designers – the Governmental Center does, none the less, make a strong statement. And it also has some of the most dramatic interior spaces of any non-casino building in Las Vegas.

ADDRESS 500 South Central Parkway
CLIENT Clark County General Services Department
EXECUTIVE ARCHITECT Domingo Cambeiro, Inc.
SIZE 350,000 square feet
COST $48.5 million

North-west Las Vegas

C W Fentress J H Bradburn and Associates, PC 1985

North-west Las Vegas

C W Fentress J H Bradburn and Associates, PC 1985

United Blood Services: Blood Donation Center

The United Blood Services building was designed by prominent Las Vegas architects JMA, a 50-year-old firm with a recognisable tough, local style. Former JMA personnel have gone on to open several new firms, including Fielden; Holmes Sabatini; Lucchesi Galati.

Located on West Charleston Boulevard, the busy commercial strip, leading from downtown towards the western mountains, the United Blood Services: Blood Donation Center is a very austere building that is highly respected by local architects (doubtless thirsting for less to be more) and seems to represent the pragmatic and unpretentious nature of Las Vegas.

It is a dry composition of gunmetal-grey, concrete-block, horizontal and vertical planes that intersect and extend to form canopies, deep overhangs and *brises-soleil*. The entrance-way is announced by a metal-panel wall which slices into the heart of the building, separating the large, open lobby area from the administrative wing. The overall sombreness is relieved by a dash of red in the neon beating-heart logo, and the i-sections used in the canopy and joinery.

A xeriscaped internal courtyard and xeriscaped front flowerbed are in keeping with the no-nonsense aridity of this building.

CLIENT United Blood Services
ADDRESS 6930 West Charleston Boulevard
STRUCTURAL ENGINEER Mendenhall Smith Inc.
SIZE 12,000 square feet

North-west Las Vegas

JMA Architects 1992

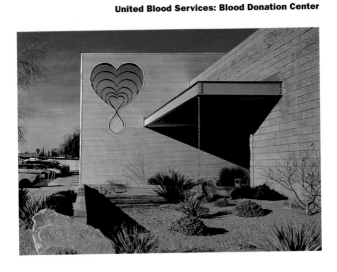

JMA Architects 1992

Siegfried and Roy's House

The main thing we know about the home of Siegfried and Roy (master illusionists and white-tiger tamers whose glitzy show plays nightly at the Mirage) is that we can't possibly know all there is to know about the place since Siegfried and Roy have just the kind of tall walls around their place that you'd expect any self-respecting celeb to have in order to ensure a little privacy.

However, you can get a pretty good glimpse of the roof line and a few clear shots through the wrought-iron gates emblazoned with Siegfried and Roy's initials. The bell tower, projecting vigas and the cross embedded in the wall make the place look like it was inspired by one of the missions of the Southwest, and reinterpreted as a kind of Mission Impossible.

Siegfried and Roy magic seems responsible for a number of eccentric elements, such as the white cement palm trees in pots that appear to have been left on the roof.

North-west Las Vegas

ADDRESS 1639 Valley Drive (at Vegas Drive)
ACCESS can be glimpsed from outside

Household Credit Card Service Center

There aren't enough buildings like the Household Credit Card Service Center in Las Vegas. Its planning and design are strong and simple, bold without being pretentious. It is planned around a generously dimensioned interior courtyard that gives a real focus and centre to the building. This is a feature that clearly would make the building more enjoyable to use on a daily basis. Within the context of Summerlin, a new masterplanned community in north-west Las Vegas, it is a largely symmetrical, four-square façade facing Banbury Cross Drive.

The Center is monumental in its massing, as is appropriate for a 140,000-square-foot office building in a planned community, where these freestanding office buildings take on some of the civic import that was once more likely to have been associated with public buildings. The 4-foot-square sandstone panels give the façade of the building weight and presence. At the same time, the tall, arched section of glass in the centre of the façade is welcoming, opening up the privatised interior of the office building to the public and clearly denoting entry.

ADDRESS 10,000 Banbury Cross Drive
CLIENT The Howard Hughes Corporation
EXECUTIVE ARCHITECT JMA Architects
STRUCTURAL ENGINEER Martin & Peltyn, Inc.
SIZE 140,000 square feet

Jerome Kassavan Associates

North-west Las Vegas

Jerome Kassavan Associates

Outside Las Vegas

Stateline: Interstate 15 at the Nevada/California Stateline 206
Hoover Dam 210

Stateline: Interstate 15 at the Nevada/California Stateline

WHISKEY PETE'S HOTEL AND CASINO (1970s–present)
BUFFALO BILL'S RESORT AND CASINO (1994)
PRIMADONNA RESORT AND CASINO (1990)

Since so many visitors approach Vegas from California, we didn't feel we had a lot of choice about whether or not to include this entry. After all, it sits right across the California border and provides a real taste of genuine Las Vegas theming and action before you even get to Las Vegas.

How can you pass up a development comprising three different resorts, in the middle of nowhere, that manages to put a monorail across a highway? At Stateline, cacti and sand stand cheek by jowl with futurism. The monorail is only 1700 feet long, and representative of the way in which this kind of transit system has been used to date in Las Vegas – as a tourist attraction or ride as much as a way of getting people around.

The three establishments at Stateline are all owned by Primadonna Resorts, Inc. Whiskey Pete's began as a little two-pump gas station and coffee shop, a bar and a dozen or so slot machines in the mid 1950s. The 18-storey hotel and casino has a somewhat nominal castle theme, and boasts the original Bonnie and Clyde Death Car and the restored Dutch Schultz, Al Capone's Gangster Car.

Our favourite of the three complexes is Buffalo Bill's, home of the Desperado (billed as the tallest and fastest roller coaster in the world, along with what must surely be the only 16-storey high-rise in the world built to resemble a giant, red wooden shed. It is in perfect scale for the vastness of the surrounding desert (though one wonders just how long

the land around Stateline will remain undeveloped). The big shed and the roller coaster look terrific together.

The Primadonna's theming is nineteenth-century country club-cum-resort hotel. Even though it's too hot to want to be outside, any Vegas hotel of only three or four storeys, with tiered exterior circulation treated as porches or galleries, nonetheless has an inherently friendlier quality than a high-rise building type with internal circulation.

Hoover Dam

If you are going to Las Vegas to see one of the man-made wonders of the world, a stunning example of human enterprise, ingenuity and artistry, which would you choose: the Boylesque female impersonator review, magician Lance Burton floating a naked woman in the air – or the Hoover Dam? We'll leave you to fight that out with your conscience, but in order to help you make your decision, a few words about the marvels of Hoover Dam.

It is an engineering marvel due to its site alone, one of such isolation that power had to be brought in all the way from San Bernardino, California, 320 miles away, and the nearest real town was Las Vegas, some 40 miles away. The mighty Colorado River had to be diverted around the site during its construction. The resulting structure, built of some 40 million cubic yards of concrete, is one of the chief monuments of the FDR administration's public works programme. Public buildings from this era in the US often had an incredible sense of weight and mass in their walls (not unlike the Hoover Dam) – a sense of architecture made of mighty slab-like masses piled up against one another and then chipped away in layers, of bulwarks expressing a sense of barely-contained strength.

LOCATION Interstate 93 south,
from Nevada to Arizona
CLIENT Department of the Interior,
Bureau of Reclamation
CHIEF DESIGNER John Savage
BUILDER Six Companies, Inc.

John Savage 1935

Outside Las Vegas

John Savage 1935

Index

Ad-Art Inc. 42, 62, 74, 98, 132, 162
Aladdin **42**
Albers-Gruen Associates 50
Archigram 86
Architecture By Five
  Nevada Power Company
    Administrative Headquarters
    158
Arquitectonica 160
Atlandia Design 60, 64

Babe's Italian Ices **156**
Baldwin and Kranzlin 92
Bally's Las Vegas 6
Bally's Las Vegas, Bally's Plaza **44–46**
Barbary Coast **52**
Barnard, Charles 42, 62, 164
Barragán, Luis 13, 168
Barton Myers Associates
  University of Nevada at Las Vegas,
    College of Architecture – Phase 1
    126–128
Bellagio 38
Bennett, William 10
Bergman, Joel 62, 66
Betsky, Aaron 26
Boneyard **162–166**
Bookmart **94**
Boulder City 15
Boulder Dam, *see* Hoover Dam
Boulevard Hotel **94**
Bronson, Skip 72
Buffalo Bill's Resort and Casino 15,
  206
Burton, Lance 210

C W Fentress J H Bradburn and
  Associates
  Clark County Governmental Center
    194–196
Caesars Forum shops **50**
Caesars Palace 6, 9, 11, 48–50, 86
Campbell & Campbell 44
Candela, Felix 78
Carousel Gift Shop 78
Carpenter Sellers Associates
  Flower Peddler, The **118**
Castaways 9
Castleman, Deke 68, 82
Chanin, Paul 114
Charleston Boulevard 10
Chrisotomo, Rudy 164
Circus Circus 9, **86–88**
Circus Circus Enterprises, Inc. 24, 28
Clark County Governmental Center **194–196**
Clark County Library and Performing
  Arts Center **122**
Claude, Georges 162
Colorado River 210
La Concha Motel 11, **78**
Conversano, Henry 62
El Cortez 52, 98
Crisostomo, Rudy 168
Cunningham Hamilton Quinter 92

Daly, Leo A 140
  Barbary Coast **52**
Debbie Reynolds Museum 136
Defence Housing Corporation 12
Degraff, Scott 132

Department of Motor Vehicles, West
  Flamingo Office 13, **172–174**
Desert Inn 9
Devroude, Tony 32
Dive! Las Vegas **72**
DMJM Las Vegas 13
  Las Vegas City Hall Complex **188**
Domingo Cambeiro, Inc. 196
Donald W Reynolds Center (UNLV)
  124
Doriot, Fred
  Holiday Inn Boardwalk Casino **40**
Dougall Design Associates, Inc. 50
  Monte Carlo **38**
Drink … and Eat Too! 12, **132–134**
Duell Corporation 36
Dworsky Associates 7

Edwards, Dan 88, 164
Elbasani & Logan Architects
  Gold Key Shops, The **80**
EME Entertainment, Inc. 40, 50
Excalibur 7, 10, 11, **26–28**, 168

Federal Sign 82, 162, 164
Ferguson's Downtown Motel **96**
First Security Bank **144**
Flamingo Hilton 9, **54–56**
Flamingo Library, *see* Clark County
  Library and Performing Arts Center
Flower Peddler, The **118**
Franklin D Israel Design Associates
  Hard Rock Casino and Hotel **130**
Franklin, Tom and Albert
  Ferguson's Downtown Motel **96**

Fremont Street 10, 11
Fremont Street Experience **98–104**, 164
Friedmutter & Associates
  Bally's Las Vegas, Bally's Plaza **44–46**
Frontier 9

G C Wallace, Inc.
  Hilton Country Club **116**
Gaskin & Bezanski
  New York New York **30**
Gaughan, Jackie 52, 98
Gaughan, Michael 52
Gehry, Frank O 120
Gensler Associates Architects 36
Gerald Garapich & Associates
  Drink … and Eat Too! **132–134**
Gilbert, Ned 156
Glitter Gulch 102
Gold Key Shops, The **80**
Golden Nugget 98
Graves, Michael 12, 122, 160
Greenbaum, Gus 82
Grossman, Melvin 50

Hacienda Hotel and Casino 20
Hadid, Zaha 160
Hammargren, Lonny 12
  Lonny Hammargren House **120**
Hard Rock Casino and Hotel 12, **130**
Harrah's **70**
Harry Campbell Architects 7
Heath and Company 162, 164
  Flamingo Hilton **54–56**
Henderson 12, 144, 148
Hess, Alan 96

Las Vegas: a guide to recent architecture

Hilton Country Club **116**
Hoffa, Jimmy 48
Holiday Casino, *see* Harrah's
Holiday Inn Boardwalk Casino **40**
Holmes Sabatini Associates 12
    Student Services Building, University of
    Nevada, Las Vegas **124**
Holmes Sabatini Associates Architects
    Department of Motor Vehicles, West
    Flamingo Office ??**–174**
    Whitney Library **150**
Homer Rissman and Associates 70
Honnold and Russell 96
    Flamingo Hilton **54–56**
Honnold, Douglas 54
Hoover Dam 8, 15, **210**
Horizon High School **178–180**
Houseal, Barry 156
Household Credit Card Service Center
    14, **202**
Howard Hughes Corporation 14
Howard, George Thomas 36
HSA Architects, *see* Holmes Sabatini
    Associates
Huetting and Schrom 50
Hughes, Howard 6, 9, 14, 68
Hunsberger, Charles 190

Interstate 15 **206–208**

Jack Miller Associates
    Stardust **74–76**
Jerde Partnership, Inc., The 11, 62, 64
    Fremont Street Experience **98–104**
Jerde, Jon 100

Jeremy Railton & Associates 28, 100
Jerome Kassavan Associates
    Household Credit Card Service Center
    202
JMA Architects 14, 122, 202
    United Blood Services, Blood Donation
    Center **198**
Joe's E-Z Bail Bonds 94
Judd, Robert Stacy 184
Judson Studios 32
Julius Gabriele AIA & Associates
    Las Vegas Country Club **112**

Katzenberg, Jeffrey 72
Kerkorian, Kirk 44
Kimsey, Windom 140, 146, 178

Larsen, Jack, Sr 164
Las Vegas Boulevard, *see* Strip, The
Las Vegas City Hall Complex 13, **188**
Las Vegas Country Club 12, **112**
Las Vegas Library/Lied Discovery
    Children's Museum 13, **190–192**
Las Vegas McCarron International
    Airport 140
Las Vegas Temple-Church of Jesus Christ
    of Latter Day Saints 184
Las Vegas Temple-Church of Jesus Christ
    of Latterday Saints 14
Last Frontier Hotel and Casino 20
Legoretta, Ricardo 116
Leming, Brian 52, 68, 84
Lemoine, Mark 116
Levy, John 46
Liberace Museum 12, **136–138**

Liberace Plaza 12
Linton, Lee
  Aladdin **42**
Little Church of the West **20**
Lonny Hammargren House **120**
Luckman and Pereira 54
Luxor, The 7, 10, **22–24**, 168

Marie Antoinette building 132
Marnell Corrao Associates, Inc. 28, 48,
  50, 62, 84
  Rio Hotel and Casino **168–170**
  Sands Hotel and Casino **68**
Marnell, Anthony A 168
Martin & Peltyn, Inc. 122, 158, 184, 192,
  202
Martin, Dean 68
McAllister, Wayne
  Sands Hotel and Casino **68**
McCarron International Airport 12
Meisel Associates Ltd
  Dive! Las Vegas **72**
Mendenhall Smith Inc. 92, 198
Meyer, Scherer & Rockcastle, Ltd
  Sahara West Library and Museum **160**
MGM Grand Hotel, Casino and Theme
  Park 10, **34–36**, 44
Michael Graves Architect
  Clark County Library and
    Performing Arts Center **122**
Miller, Paul 74, 164
Mint 98
Mirage, The 10, 11, **58–62**
Monte Carlo **38**–??
Moore, Bill

Little Church of the West **20**
Mormons 14, 184
Morris Brown and Associates
  Harrah's **70**
Morton, Michael 132
Murder, Inc. 9

Nellis Airforce Base 8
Nelson, Gary
  Stratosphere Tower **90–92**
Neon Museum, *see* Boneyard 164
Nervi, Pier Luigi 78
Nevada Power Company Administrative
  Headquarters **158**
New York New York **30**, 156
Newton, Wayne 42, 136
North Las Vegas Airport 9
Northern Club 98

Olio Design 64
Orleans 52

Par-A-Dice Inn **106**
Pelli, Cesar 160
Perini Building Company 70
Predock, Antoine 13, 116, 160, 194
  Las Vegas Library/Lied Discovery
    Children's Museum **190–192**
Presley, Elvis 6, 42
Primadonna Resort and Casino 15,
  206

El Rancho Vegas Motel 106
Regency Towers **114**
Rio Hotel and Casino 13, **168–170**

Las Vegas: a guide to recent architecture

Rissman & Rissman Associates 132
    Circus Circus **86–88**
    Regency Towers **114**
Riviera 11, **82**
Rodriguez, Paul 164
Rodriguez, Raul 54
Rossi, Aldo 13, 160
Russell, George Vernon 54

Sahara Club 116
Sahara West Library and Museum **160**
Sam's Town **152**
Sands Hotel and Casino 9, **68**
Sarno, Jay 9, 48, 58, 86
Satellite D Project, McCarron
    International Airport **140**
Savage, John
    Hoover Dam **210**
Scott-Brown, Denise 144
Siegel, Benjamin 'Bugsy' 9, 54, 58
Siegfried and Roy 22, 60, 62
Siegfried and Roy's House **200**
Sign Systems, Inc. 70, 162
Simpson, Veldon 13
    Excalibur **26–28**
    Luxor, The **22–24**
    MGM Grand Hotel, Casino and Theme
        Park **34–36**
    Veldon Simpson's House **142**
Sinatra, Frank 6, 68
Six Companies, Inc. 210
Spielberg, Steven 72
Stardust 11, **74–76**
Stardust Hotel 170

Stateline 40
Statue of Liberty **156**
Stern, Martin, Jr 68, 96
    Bally's Las Vegas, Bally's Plaza **44–46**
Steve's Buy and Sell Jewelry **94**
Stone, Warwick 130
Stratosphere Tower 40, **90–92**
Streets, etc
    Banbury Cross Drive 202
    Bel-Air Drive 114
    Boulder Highway 152
    Cameron Street 166
    East Charleston 182
    East Desert Inn Road 116
    East Flamingo Road 118, 122
    East Fremont Street 96
    East Harmon Avenue 134
    East Tropicana 150
    East Tropicana Avenue 138
    Fashion Show Mall 72
    Fremont Street 106
    Joe Brown Drive 112
    Las Vegas Boulevard 72
    Las Vegas Boulevard North 192
    Las Vegas Boulevard South 20, 24, 30,
        32, 36, 38, 40, 42, 46, 52, 56, 62, 66,
        68, 70, 78, 80, 82, 84, 88, 92
    Liberace Plaza 138
    Liberty Square 156
    North Las Vegas Avenue 152
    North Valley Road 144
    Paradise Road 130, 140
    Ridgecrest 120
    Sandhill Road 120
    South Central Parkway 196

Streets, etc (continued)
  South Maryland Parkway 110
  Stewart Avenue 188
  Temple View Drive 184
  Tomyasu 142
  Valley Drive 200
  Valley Verde Court 148
  West Charleston Boulevard 198
  West Flamingo 170, 174
  West Harmon Avenue 180
  West Sahara 158, 160
  West Tropicana Avenue 52
Strip, The 7, 10, 11, 13
Strip, the 64, 78, 86, 94, 98
Student Services Building, University
  of Nevada, Las Vegas 124
Stupak, Bob 90
Summerlin 14, 202
Swisher & Hall Ltd 126, 192
  First Security Bank 144

Tally-Ho Motel, seeAladdin
Tate & Snyder Architects 12, 13, 14,
  160
  Horizon High School 178–180
  Las Vegas Temple-Church of Jesus
    Christ of Latter Day Saints 184
  Satellite D Project, McCarron
    International Airport 140
  Tate & Snyder Offices 146–148
Tate & Snyder Offices 146–148
Thomas, Roger 60, 66
Thompson, Hunter S 6, 120
TRA 140
Treasure Island 7, 10, 11, **64–66**

Tropicana, The **32**

United Blood Services, Blood Donation
  Center **198**
University of Nevada at Las Vegas (UNLV)
  12
University of Nevada at Las Vegas,
  College of Architecture – Phase 1
  126–128
US Bank 14, **182**

Vanity Park **110**
Vegas Vickie 164
Veldon Simpson's House **142**
Venturi, Robert 144
Virtualand 24

Wayne, Kermit 164
Weeks, Steve 164
Westward Ho **84**
Whiskey Pete's Hotel and Casino 15,
  206
White, Gene
  Statue of Liberty **156**
Whitney Library **150**
Wilkerson, Billy 9
Williams, Marge 82, 164
Williams, Paul
  Carousel Gift Shop 78
  La Concha Motel **78**
Wolfe, Tom 54, 162
Wright, Frank Lloyd 142
Wurster, William 106
Wynn, Steve 10, 11, 58, 62, 64, 72, 86,
  98, 100

Las Vegas: a guide to recent architecture

Yates-Silverman, Inc. 40, 52
YESCO 14, 48, 52, 68, 84, 88, 98, 100,
   162–166, 168
Young Electric Sign Company, *see* YESCO

Zelner, Joseph 114
Zukov, Nikita 82
Zunino Associates 174

Las Vegas: a guide to recent architecture